Leadership

Random Thoughts of Leadership, Strategies, Global Business, and Spirituality – A Collection of Essays.

Dr. Saju Skaria

Copyright © 2018 Dr. Saju Skaria

All rights reserved. No part of this book may be used or reproduced by any means, graphic, electronic, or mechanical, including photocopying, recording, taping, or by any information storage retrieval system, without the written permission of the copyright owner and publisher of this book except in the case of brief quotations embodied in critical articles and reviews. In the event you use any of the information in this book for yourself or others, the author and the publisher assume no responsibility for your actions.

Although every precaution has been taken to verify the accuracy of the information contained herein, the author and publisher assume no responsibility for any errors or omissions. No liability is assumed for damages that may result from the use of information contained within.

To my wife, Shiny,
who's always accepted me for who I'm and supported my hustle, drive, and ambition: you are and always will be my perfect wife and mother to our lovely children, Rinku and Robin.

"All who have accomplished great things have had a great aim, have fixed their gaze on a goal which was high, one which sometimes seemed impossible."
-Orison Sweet Marden

Preface

I grew up in a village in Kerala, India in an agricultural family with limited means but with unlimited love and care. I was the fifth among six siblings. Education was the central theme that was running in my family. I have seen firsthand the challenges faced by my parents for raising funds for supporting our scholastic needs. So, early in my childhood I understood the value of education. I continued to be a lifelong learner and acquired several academic credentials including a Doctorate.

Fast forward, now I live in one of the best countries on planet earth, The United States of America. For me, this is the give back time to pass on the best I have I acquired for over three decades while serving in military, government, and global corporations at various leadership roles.

"Random Thoughts of Leadership, Strategies, Global Business, and Spirituality – A Collection of Essays" is an assortment of snippets that I wrote in a lucid fashion to benefit readers of all categories. Hope you will enjoy the book.

Dr. Saju Skaria
Phoenix, AZ, USA.

Contents

On Race, Minorities, and Social Change!..8
Thoughtful prayers and prayerful thoughts!..10
ABC of Life!...12
How to stay focused!...17
The Second Coming!..19
Create the Life You Want!...21
On God, Faith, and Immortality!...22
Are Leaders Change Agents?..24
Organizational Dynamic Models..26
Holistic or Systems Thinking for Organizational Growth........................28
Business Ethics and Leadership...32
Global Business Operating Strategy..37
Leadership in Troubled Times!...43
Smile When You Bleed!...46
Global Leader Roles..48
Offshore Centric Enterprises – 51
Communication in a Global Context...56
Ethical Issues in Information Technology...58
Goal Setting: 5 Tips for Setting Effective New Year's Resolutions...........62
Global Marketing Challenges!..64
Business Ethics!...70
Organize Your Mind to Organize Your Life!..74
Strategic Leaders!...80
Creating High Performance Organizational Culture................................83
Organizational Behavior: The Paradigm Shift..93
The Power of Habit!..99
The Success Code!...103
Words and Destiny!...106
Risk Management Strategies in the Global Environment.....................109
Some leadership thoughts in troubled times!..113
Positive Intelligence: A Game Changer...116
The First Person You Must Lead is YOU..120
New Year – Yes, You Can!!..122
My Marathon Story...124
Five Universal Citizens..127
Digital Twins..130
Corporate World - Do You Really Care?..133
Breaking the Glass Ceiling...136

How the "Big History" Shaping my Thinking and Writing. 138
Ingredients of High Performance 140
Coaching for Leaders 141
A Constant Leadership Reminder 143
Live the "Future" Today 145
Skeptical Cat 146
Leadership and Self-Management 147
Business Optimization Approaches in a Global Context 148
Author Biography 162

On Race, Minorities, and Social Change!

The shooting death of Trayvon Martin by George Zimmerman brought in new discussions on the underlying issues of race, minorities, and related social challenges. For those readers outside of the United States, this is a hotly debated issue in the US that in a way was disturbing the social fabric of the most open society in the world.

My intent is not to discuss the right and wrong on this particular incident. My intent is to share the views on the underlying social tension. Although dominant groups seek to define the social landscape, groups who experience unequal treatment have in the past resisted power and seek significant social change and continue to do so today. The sweeping changes happening around world including the "Arab Spring" is part of this fight against the social oppression.

Race is a social construction, and this process benefits the oppressor, who defines who is privileged and who is not. The acceptance of race in a society as a legitimate category allows racial hierarchies to emerge to the benefit of the dominant "races." Racism is a doctrine of racial supremacy that states one race is superior to another. One CNN contributor commented, "Stating that there is no racism is the new racism". We cannot ignore the reality, but need to work closely to address them. Coming to minorities; a social minority need not be a mathematical one. A minority group is a subordinate group whose members has significantly less control or powers over their own lives than do the members of a dominant or majority group. Why minorities join as a block and typically forming vote banks? This is part of survival instinct; a rule applicable around the world. The problem comes when some "messiahs" arrive as leaders of these minorities with nothing but self-interest and take advantage of the minorities and socially deprived. Hope many of my readers outside of US can relate the issues which are relevant to your own environment.

The need of the hour is a pluralistic society. Pluralism describes a society in which several different groups coexist, with no dominant or subordinate groups. People individually chose what cultural patterns to keep and which to let go. The two significant forces that are absent in a truly pluralistic society are prejudice and discrimination. For many, this looks like a distant dream, but human race has remarkable agility and the days are not far off when such dreams are realized!

Thoughtful prayers and prayerful thoughts!

I am a Christian and I share my views from a Christian perspective. Since I was born and raised in India prior to migrating to U.S., my thoughts are also deeply influenced by the Eastern and Hindu spirituality.

What's prayer? Prayer is a communion and communication with the higher being. And, why we pray? Prayer heals. The more we learn about technology and develop our skills, we also learn about the uncertainties and human limitations. Prayer and faith can remove human limitations. It helps one accept reality without pains. Holy Bible says, "Come to Me, all of you who are weary and carry heavy burdens, and I will give you rest" (Matthew 11:28).

In the Eastern and Hindu culture, prayer and meditation plays a central role. One of the oldest forms of meditation reported in human history is in Hindu Vedas, dated back to 15th century BCE. Subsequently, meditation spread in the Taoist China and Buddhist India around 5th and 6th century BCEs by the influence of the Vedas.

The repetitive, rhythmic chants and offerings have its own healing power. Religious practices like Orthodox Christians, Jews, Hindus, Buddhists, and Taoists follow this tradition. There are several references on mediation and prayer; hâgâ (means to sigh or murmur, but also to meditate) in Hebrew Bible, dhyaana in Buddhism and in Hinduism are two typical examples.

Atheists may have a concern on prayer to a higher being. But they can always focus on meditation which is generally an inwardly oriented, personal practice, which individuals do by themselves.

During Lenten time for Christian around the world; preparation of the believer—through prayer, penance, repentance, almsgiving, and self-denial. Let it not be a ritual. Let's offer the best to the world, selflessly.

ABC of Life!

ABC (Avoid Bad Company) in Life. Your life's happiness depends a lot on the company you keep. Diane McLaren, a popular holistic health practitioner, coach & trainer uncovered patterns and strategies to keep a happy life. Practice these easy strategies in order to improve happiness and become more upbeat and optimistic. The following are her recommendations to lead a healthy and happy life!

1. *Avoid Emotional Vampires*

    Life's success depends a lot with the company you keep. Do you attract emotional vampires or losers into your life? Are you a loser magnet? Emotional vampires and losers literally drain our batteries, slow us down and make us upset. To become happier, optimistic and energetic — avoid emotional vampires. Emotional vampires include people who put you down, criticize or mock you, or sabotage your dreams and aspirations. Take survey of your life by making a list of people and situations you expose yourself to. Then, discard or limit people, habits or situations that keep you from feeling optimistic and happy. In other words,' burn your bridges' if needed.

2. *Detox Your Mind*

   You can detox your mind just as people detox their bodies. To get rid of negative or intruding bad thoughts, remember this "Rule of Happiness": You can only keep one thought in your mind at a time. You can focus your thoughts on either pessimistic/unhappy or optimistic/happy thoughts. It's your choice. Happy and optimistic people expect the best. When setbacks or problems pop up, focus on finding a solution. Unhappy and pessimistic people focus on complaining, but happy and optimistic people focus on solutions.

3. *Optimism and Happiness by the Numbers*

   Are you obsessed with negative thoughts that lead you to a bad mood? A simple way to become happy and optimistic is to count your way to more positive thoughts. It's easy to become an expert at switching your negative and bad thoughts to more positive and upbeat thoughts and feelings. Each time you have a negative thought, immediately switch to a positive thought or solution to your woes.

4. *Change your body posture*

   Happy and energetic individuals take big steps, walk faster and stand taller. They seem to exude an endless supply of energy. In sharp contrast, pessimistic, unhappy and lifeless people shuffle their feet, take tiny steps, walk slowly and slouch. They appear lifeless and have burned–out their batteries. Watch how you carry your body. Use the body-posture of happy, optimistic people, such as taking big steps, walking faster and standing taller. Using these techniques will help you become happy and energetic. They are easy to carry out, and will create a positive domino effect with people in your life.

5. *Watch what you say — and never say words such as "try"*

   To start acting like happy and optimistic people, you need to learn what they do. Optimistic people act and talk in certain ways and use certain words. The words people use can affect their moods and energy levels. Changing your words can actually change your attitude and feelings. Use "upbeat" words, instead of "upsetting" words. For example, "I feel overwhelmed" can seem upsetting. So instead say, "I feel challenged nevertheless I can do it" which is more upbeat. One of the most interesting differences between happy and unhappy people is that happy people rarely or even never use the word 'try' or 'but.' These two words leave people feeling hopeless and not in control of their lives. Happy people feel hopeful, and take tons of responsibility for their lives.

6. *Focus on What You Want & Not On What You Do not Want*
   Worry is the #1 happiness and energy zapper. The fastest way to fill you with endless joy and energy is to stop worrying. How can you do that? Each time you have a negative thought, immediately switch it to a positive thought such as a solution to your woes. People who focus on solutions rather than problems are optimistic, happy and very high energy.

7. *Pursue What You Love To Do and It Will Light Your Fire*
   The best way to start your day and jump out of bed with an enthusiastic mood is to find your passion. Find out what thrills you and you'll find boundless new energy to jump out of bed and start the day with a great mood. People who have no energy in the morning or even

during the day are really lost souls. They do not have a real reason to get out of bed each day. Finding your passion or what thrills you in life can turn you on each day, light your fire and boost your mood. Anyone can become more upbeat and optimistic. When people use these techniques, they invariably feel a heavy burden lift off their shoulders. They feel positive, upbeat, and confident.

You only need a few minutes to put these tips into action. They can be your key to enhanced life including your health, wealth, and career success.

Remember: Optimism is the hidden key to your personal success. Optimists possess a clear vision of an exciting life, confidently work on goals to achieve their vision, and take self-responsibility. In contrast, pessimists have no clear vision of a fantastic life, and they love to complain, blame, and moan. So which do you want to be —- happy & optimistic or unhappy and pessimistic?

Finally, follow the ABC; Avoid Bad Company, keep away from the Emotional Vampires!!

How to stay focused!

Some personal experiences pulled me completely off track. A silly work – politics spat blew my deadlines and wasted valuable time and energy. It made me think hard again on how we deal with such issues and stay productive. While we can't run away from situations, it is important how we tackle them effectively.

Prayer and meditation are strong tools to avoid distraction and stress (my wife is a big advocate on this). I always have the intent, but fail many a time. One old theory on the topic is that meditation is just like exercise: it trains the brain as if gray matter were a bundle of muscles. You work those muscles and they get stronger. And the results are clear: it's not wanting to meditate but actually meditating that improves your brain's performance. So next time, we blame on meditation, please look inward and ask the question; have we done our part correctly?

Yet another way to deal with the situation is avoid multi-tasking. While multitasking may seem to be saving time, psychologists, neuroscientists and others are finding that it can put us under a great deal of stress and actually make us less efficient. Studies by David E. Meyer, a professor of psychology at the University of Michigan, and his colleagues found that for all types of tasks, the participants lost time when they had to move back and forth from one undertaking to another, and that it took significantly longer to switch between the more complicated tasks.

In a Harvard Business Review article, Overloaded Circuits: Why Smart People Underperform, Dr. Hallowell wrote that attention deficit trait "springs entirely from the environment". "As our minds fill with noise — feckless synaptic events signifying nothing — the brain gradually loses its capacity to attend fully and gradually to anything," he wrote.
Can we manage our situation and stay focused? The answer is, yes. For that, we need to "recreate our boundaries" and "train our mind". That means not looking at your messages every 20 seconds, switching off the cellphones in meetings, and not looking at your emails while talking over the phone. Sleeping less to do more is a bad strategy.

We are efficient only when we sleep enough, eat right, exercise, and meditate. Focus on single tasking and avoid distractions. Finally, the result depends on how sincere you are with yourself.

The Second Coming!

Easter; the remembrance and celebration of Christ's resurrection. What is the message this offers to people? My previous article on the topic was read by a large number of people around the world, Christians and non-Christians, believers and non-believers. So, I will stay focused on the underlying message.

Never be the prisoner of the past. There is always opportunity for growth and make a second coming. Be the architect of the future. The resurrection is the reflection of the bouncing back. In Christian faith, had Jesus not resurrected, there is no further hope left. By rising from the dead, Jesus gave this eternal hope of rebounding even from the worst adversity.

This is also a message for people who are habitually miserable and whine about everything in life. The upbeat people have hope and aspirations and they will bounce back from adversities, more often than the failure thinkers.

How to overcome anxiety? The fear of failure is part of the process. Jesus Christ was no exception. The best way to deal with is to jump into action. Courage gives the self-control to overcome hurdles and persist on your goals where others have failed.

Most of us have read about purpose driven life. The purpose of life is a life of purpose. Our endeavor should be channelizing that purpose to bring joy and happiness to people around us. There is no magic wand to achieve this. It is an iterative and incremental approach. We fall at every stage. Our ability to get up and move forward makes the difference in our lives.
Our creative best come into play when we realize the higher purpose in life. Let the Easter be an opportunity for our second coming to realize why we are called into the universe as unique beings.

Create the Life You Want!

Is balancing work, life, and family a priority for you and how stay motivated? Susan M. Heathfield provides some insightful responses in this area. She recommends what is called Guided Thinking Exercises. Try these exercises to focus your career planning and life thinking – yes, you have to do the work to get to your goal.

1. Write down your ten favorite activities, the ones without which your life would feel bereft. No career choice is suitable unless you get to do your favorite activities at least weekly, and preferably, daily.
2. Write down the top five goals you want to accomplish in your life and career. (Think money, fame, impact, contribution and more.) Your selected career must enable you to reach these goals.
3. List everything you'd like to do in your lifetime. These lists can run several hundred items. Your chosen career must allow the accomplishment of these dreams.

On God, Faith, and Immortality!

The core of religious faith is that mystic feeling that unites man with God. It is only in relation to the Creator, and the purpose which that Creator has fixed for His creatures, that human existence has any meaning. This state of spiritual communion can be brought about and maintained by means of meditation and prayer. And this is the reason why various religions have so much stressed the importance of worship. In reality, there is only one religion, the religion of God. The purpose of God in creating man has been, and will ever be, to enable him to know his Creator and to attain His Presence.

Many people live their lives without ever reflecting on life itself or its meaning for them. Their lives may be full of activities. They may marry, have children, run a business, or become scientists or musicians, without ever obtaining any degree of understanding of why they do these things. Their lives have no overall purpose to give meaning to separate events, and they may have no clear idea of their own nature or identity, of who they really are.

The ultimate aim in life of every human soul should be to attain moral and spiritual excellence--to align one's inner being and outward behavior with the will of an all-loving Creator. That each individual has been bestowed with a unique destiny by God--a destiny which unfolds in accordance with the free exercise of the choices and opportunities presented in life. In particular, it is through the moral exercise of our divinely conferred free will that opportunities are provided for spiritual advancement.

Are Leaders Change Agents?

"We must become the change we want to see." –
Mahatma Gandhi

Leaders are change agents. Leaders should be responsible for building empowered organizations where individuals have the knowledge, skill, desire, and opportunity to personally succeed in a way that leads to collective organizational success. To succeed internationally, leaders should know why they are selling globally, how their product compares with competitors' products, what transactions are involved in selling globally, and who they can consult, contract, or hire to provide needed specialized expertise.

Glenn Llopis, Contributor for Forbes magazine put this eloquently. According to Llopis, change is the new normal for leadership success and all leaders must accept this fact.

Change management is no longer a term that denotes only operational improvements, cost efficiencies and process reengineering. Change management has become a much bigger, more interwoven part of the overall business fabric – an embedded leadership requirement that plays into everything that we do, every day, and how we go about getting things done, regardless of hierarchy or rank. In the end, every leader must be a change agent.

Leadership in the 21st century not only requires the ability to continuously manage crisis and change – but also the circular vision to see around, beneath and beyond the obvious in order to anticipate the unexpected before circumstances force your hand. As you embark upon your change management journey, here are ten things that will challenge your capabilities as a change agent and potentially become defining moments along your leadership success path.

Organizational Dynamic Models

Organizational Dynamics' domain is primarily organizational behavior and development and secondarily, HRM and strategic management. There are many models that provide an understanding of characteristics and dynamics of specific organizational disciplines. The Organization Dynamic Model presented by Rigsby links the many individual models together; so that one may understand how independent disciplines interrelate within an organization.

This model has three core drivers that must be aligned with each other in order for organizations to succeed in business. The first driver is organizational strategy, which is the blueprint of the organization. This answers questions such as what the business is doing now, and what it should be doing. The second driver is organizational design according to Rigsby states that the infrastructure imposed by management that employees must contend with in order to do their jobs. The third driver is organizational culture, which is a feeling at the company.

Rigsby adds that the culture is the outcome of the total set of beliefs, protocols, and practices that an organization maintains for prolonged periods of time. Organizations are made up of people with different thoughts and ideas, and with varying degree of potential and ability to work in individual and team environment. These individuals bring their own perceptions into the formal and informal groups within an organization. This can be beneficial in that individuals inject new ideas into the groups. However, problems can arise when assumptions clash and individuals are not managed correctly.

Holistic or Systems Thinking for Organizational Growth

Holistic or systems thinking is based on system dynamics and provides ways of understanding practical business issues (example B2B business); it looks at systems in terms of particular types of cycles (archetypes); and it includes explicit system modeling of complex issues. It's a philosophical approach that shapes the outcome of system design.

System thinking simplifies life by helping us to see the deeper patterns lying behind the events and the details. The essence of the discipline of systems thinking lies in a shift of mind:

- Seeing interrelationships rather than linear cause-effect chains, and
- Seeing processes of change rather than snapshots

Initially, systems were viewed as machines or closed-loop systems whose rigid structure defined their function. Analytical thinking fits this model well. Systems are simply the sum of their parts, assembled in defined ways to create specific behaviors. In the next stage, systems were viewed as biological creations. The biological model views systems as an open loop with single-minded, purposeful behavior. The system responds to instability in the open-loop environment by adjusting its actions to meet its defined goal. A thermostat provides a simple mechanical example of this type of system. The third stage views systems as social entities. The social model views systems as being composed of a voluntary association of purposeful entities that have their own choice of goals and the means to achieve them. But purposeful is not the same as goal seeking.

Goal seeking means that you have alternate means of achieving a single goal. Purposeful means you can change the goal as well as the means. In the social model, integration is a continual process. This process requires filling the purpose of the individual entities and aligning their fulfillment with that of the whole. Members are held together by common objectives and agreed upon ways of pursuing them. (example, Cohorts in in a business or project environment). Consensus is essential to alignment.

Openness: In his book, Systems Thinking: Managing Chaos and Complexity, Jamshid Gharajedaghi defined five system principles:
- Openness
- Purposefulness
- Multi-dimensionality

- Emergent property
- Counter-intuitiveness

Openness means the behavior of a system can only be understood in the context of its environment. Open systems are guided by a code of conduct, whether that is DNA or culture. When left alone, open systems tend to reproduce themselves. Typically, we evaluate a system's environment and identify variables that can be controlled and those that cannot. As we look at more open systems we might identify environmental variables that can at least be influenced if not controlled. Why openness is important: We need to look at business as an open system with different variables. And, the inter-relationship of these variables can be influenced, if not controlled. This is where the openness becomes relevant for the business context. Business undergoes constant changes and that requires more sophisticated systems to meet constantly changing business needs.

Customer relationship context: The openness is very crucial in customer relationship context. Let me explain this with an analogy. Chaos theory states that the fluttering of a butterfly in far away in Asia can influence the weather in America. What this shows the importance of the influence of a smallest event on the final outcome. Customer is a key environment variable in system thinking and can definitely influence the outcome of business.

Productive organizations will have an open approach that encourages innovation, creativity, and system thinking. S organization spends substantial sum of money for constantly re-invent itself and system thinking is one of the key aspects of this approach.

Business Ethics and Leadership

How does one link between business ethics and leadership? American Heritage Dictionary defines ethics as the moral quality of a course of action; any set of moral principles or values; the study of the general nature of morals and of the specific moral choices to be made by the individual in his [or her] relationship with others. Business ethics is a subset of the study of ethics and is defined as the study of what makes up good and bad business conduct. This conduct occurs when the firm acts as an organization, as well as when individual managers make decisions inside the organization.

Examining what comprises the organizational culture should reveal some key attributes that encourage ethical behavior. Scholars who studied organizational reputation maintained that a positive reputation, such as one for ethical behavior, had a beneficial effect in the marketplace. Stormer credited neoclassical economic theory with the idea that ethical corporate behavior enhanced profitability, but called for a theory that encouraged ethical behavior from a philosophical standpoint of benefit to society. The sum total of individual employees' ethical values influences corporate conduct, especially in a corporation's early years. The activities during these years, in turn, form the basis of what constitutes a corporate culture, or an environment for doing business. In a free-market society, values of productivity, efficiency, and profits become part of the culture of all companies.

Theories of ethical thought

Consequential theories

Ethicists, business people, and workers who adhere to a consequential theory of ethics judge acts as ethically good or bad based on whether the acts have achieved their desired results. The actions of a business or any other societal unit are looked at as right or wrong only in terms of whether the results can be rationalized. This theory is best exemplified by the utilitarian school of thought, which is divided into two sub-schools: act utilitarianism and rule utilitarianism. In general, adherents of this school judge all conduct of individuals or businesses on whether it brings net happiness or pleasure to a society. They judge an act ethically correct after adding up the risks (unhappiness) and the benefits (happiness) to society and obtaining a net outcome.

Act utilitarian determine if an action is right or wrong on the basis of whether that individual act (the payment of a bribe) alone brings net happiness to the society as opposed to whether other alternatives (e.g., not paying the bribe or allowing others to pay the bribe) would bring more or less net happiness. Rule utilitarians argue that an act (the payment of the bribe) is ethically right if the performance of similar acts by all similar agents (other contractors) would produce the best results in society or has done so in the past. Rule utilitarians hold the position that whatever applicable rule has been established by political representatives must be followed and should serve as a standard in the evaluation of similar acts.

Deontological theories

Deontology is derived from a Greek word meaning "duty." For advocates of deontology, rules and principles determine whether actions are ethically good or bad. The consequences of individual actions are not considered. The Golden Rule, "Do unto others as you would have them do unto you," is the hallmark of the theory. Absolute deontology claims that actions can be judged ethically good or bad on the basis of absolute moral principles arrived at by human reason regardless of the consequences of an action; that is, regardless of whether there is net happiness. Immanuel Kant (1724–1804) provided an example of an absolute moral principle in his widely studied "categorical imperative." He stated that a person ought to engage only in acts that he or she could see becoming a universal standard.

Humanist theories

A third school of thought, the humanist school, evaluates actions as ethically good or bad depending on what they contribute to improving inherent human capacities such as intelligence, wisdom, and self-restraint.

Profit-oriented theory

The profit-oriented theory of social responsibility begins with a market-oriented concept of the firm that most readers were exposed to in their first or second course in economics. Holders of this theory argue that business entities are distinct organizations in our society and that their sole purpose is to increase profits for shareholders. Businesses are to be judged solely on criteria of economic efficiency and how well they contribute to growth in productivity and technology. Corporate social responsibility is shown by managers who maximize profits for their shareholders, who, in turn, are able to reinvest such profits, providing for increased productivity, new employment opportunities, and increased consumption of goods.

Managerial theory

Advocates of the managerial theory of social responsibility argue that businesses, particularly large institutions, have a number of interest groups or constituents both internally and externally that they must deal with regularly, not just stockholders and a board of directors. A business has employees, customers, suppliers, consumers, activist groups, government regulators, and others that influence decision making and the ability of the entity to make profits.

Global Business Operating Strategy

The growing trend towards globalization brings opportunities for companies to expand overseas and grow revenues. As many companies have experienced, expanding the geographic scope of the market can indeed offer rewarding growth opportunities. However, expanding to new geographic market offers serious challenges to companies. In particular, attractive markets are hardest to penetrate, as incumbents or existing competition will fight back to defend their market position.

Bryce and Dryer propose a low profile and indirect business positioning to penetrate attractive market, so as not to catch attention of existing competition until it's too late for them to react. The authors propose three business positioning approach in pursuing attractive markets, which compose of leveraging existing strengths and resources, reconfiguring the value chains by changing activities or sequence of activities in delivering value to customers, establish niches attracting customers in the fringe segments. Given the need for a global perspective in business positioning business gurus Gupta and Govindarajan recommend that companies consider the star framework of global competitive advantage. The star framework recommends that the companies select the business positioning that contributes in improving global competitive advantage of the company in terms of expanded global activity architecture, maximized location competencies, and improvement of global coordination.

Mergers and Acquisitions

Marzulli and Haskamp mentioned that there has been an increase in mergers and acquisitions activities in Northern America and worldwide. In particular, there have been significant acquisition activities done by private equity firms through leveraged buyout. The strong leveraged buy-out activities were fueled by low interest rates during the past years. However, the recent trend of increasing interest rates is creating challenges to private equity firms, as this increases their cost to acquire companies.

The intention of pursuing mergers and acquisitions is to attain synergies between companies. However, it is disturbing that only 20% of completed mergers and acquisitions are able to achieve the intended level of synergies. As the cultural difference between companies increase, the higher is the risk that such mergers and acquisitions will not yield the required results. This makes mergers and acquisition involving companies based in different countries to be more challenging.

Atkinson and Clarke point to the destructive effect of culture divide in hindering business integration post the merger and acquisition. In order for the merger and acquisition to work will require that a unified culture of the combined organization be shaped to deliver outstanding values to all stakeholders. This then requires companies to conduct pre-merger and pre-acquisition analysis that goes beyond the financial aspect to include the organizational culture perspective.

Best Practice in Global Acquisition

Cisco Systems demonstrates successful formula for global acquisitions that is worthy of emulation. Global acquisition has been an integral part of the company's operation and business model. Acquiring technology companies at a fast pace allows Cisco to absorb new technology, acquire top technical talents, increase the company's product portfolio, and neutralize upcoming competitors. Cisco acquires companies in different parts of the world to capture not only new products, but the best engineering and entrepreneurial talents as well. Upon completion of the acquisition, Cisco gives the acquired organization autonomy to operate independently. The 2004 annual report of Cisco Systems mentioned that the company completed twelve acquisitions during that year, and expected to follow the same rate of acquisitions the next year.

Chang, Chatman, and O'Reilly mentioned that the two key factors instilled in Cisco' culture serving as the foundation for its successful acquisitions are not adapting technology religion, and listening carefully to customer. Cisco did not rigidly impose one technology to the customer; instead, the organization listens to the needs and problems of the customer, and matches this with appropriate technology solution. Likewise, Chang, Chatman, and O'Reilly also mentioned that Cisco's culture is based on the principles of open communication, empowerment, trust, and integrity. Such form of organizational culture is able to support Cisco's acquisition efforts.

Strategic Partnership

Companies seek to establish strategic partnership to look for synergies in cost, capital, revenue, and growth for mutual benefit. Strategic partnership can only exist by sustaining relationship that is mutually beneficial for both parties. Likewise, a key factor influencing partnership and collaboration is the desire to maintain such relationship between the involved companies. Partnership requires the highest level of relationship, needed for industries characterized as complicated, fast changing, and rapidly developing. Larzelere and Huston further emphasized that trust is the prerequisite for developing long-term commitments. Trust serves as the foundation for nurturing and sustaining strategic partnership that requires time to build, but can be quickly damage due to miscommunication, lack of business integrity, and conflicting objectives.

Global Alliances

Colteryahn and Davis describe the evolving global environment as having increasing uncertainty, increasing global interdependence and competition, and increasing rate of change. The challenges from such an environment can be too much for an organization to face alone by itself. Such environmental trends point to the need for companies to collaborate with partners and even with competitors at a global scale. The ability of companies to build collaborative advantage will help those companies thrive in the ever increasingly complex environment. Global alliance was popularly adapted by different industries, ranging from the high technology sector to the airline industry. Global companies form alliance with foreign partners, channel partners, or even with competitors to share risk, share assets, and eventually share the pie of the market. Gupta and Govindarajan mentioned that based on the theory of cross border scalability, the risk of success of global strategy increases as the level of local infrastructure and local adaptation increases.

The formation of global alliance is the recommended mode of entry when the level of local infrastructure and local adaptation increases. Alliance will be able to leverage the strengths and assets of local partners reducing the risk and capital investment by the company. However, the challenges for global alliance pertains to the complexity of managing the relationship with alliance members due to conflicting goals, and the company's lack of control in dictating the pace of the global expansion.

Leadership in Troubled Times!

Here are few thoughts on leadership that will help you address during the troubled times. In today's busy world, we may not find enough time to do everything, but certainly can find sufficient time to do the most important things.

1. Successful people are long term thinkers. They understand how their short term actions affect long term goals. They work every day to achieve their goals.
2. The world will only give what you prepared to receive. The way you see inside of you will be the person you become outside. Be kind, honest and firm.
3. Circumstances do not make a person, that only reveal the true colors of that person.
4. Pain is inevitable, but suffering is optional. Take personal responsibility, blaming is escapism.
5. Don't live in the past, live the moment and plan for the future. You can't go back in time, but can leverage the experience for a better present and future.
6. You are the sum total of the people around you. So choose wisely and keep away from emotional vampires.

7. Speak up, don't let someone blackmail you. You move on, people will realize what they missed over a period of time.

Smile When You Bleed!

This may look very funny for many people. But, how do you respond to the most difficult question when someone is fully aware that you are bleeding? You offer an unconditional smile. Smiling is the secret to health and serenity according to several spiritual traditions. The Inner Smile practice propounds that when we smile like a Buddha, the world beams back.

A deep inner smile spreads like a relaxing elixir making us receptive to transform negative energy into positive. Conversely, a scowl suppresses our immune system by increasing stress, contracting channels and blocking energy. Research by French physiologist Dr Israel Waynbaum indicates that facial muscles used to express emotion trigger specific brain neurotransmitters. Smiling signals happy healing hormones such as ecstatic endorphins and immune boosting killer T-cells whereas frowning triggers the secretion of stress hormones. Smile therapy actually lowers the stress hormones cortisol, adrenalin and noradrenaline and produces hormones which stabilize blood pressure, relax muscles, improve respiration, reduce pain, accelerate healing and stabilize mood.

If you're feeling down the stress hormones secreted with a scowl may increase blood pressure, weaken the immune system, increase susceptibility to infections, and exacerbate depression and anxiety.

But what if we don't feel like smiling? Can we fake it till we make it? Though a heart-felt smile has a deeper effect, even a surface smile tricks the brain into releasing happy hormones according to facial biofeedback research. And the more we smile, the more we want to smile concluded a study where people allowed to smile found cartoons funnier than those suppressed from smiling by holding pencils in their lips. This is because each time we smile we reinforce happy neural pathways that fire more spontaneously with each subsequent use. Self-love smiling circuits then release healing nectar and self-hate messages release poisons that breed disease according to Taoism.

A challenge many experience in practicing the inner smile is the tendency towards negativity. We can catch an inner frown from others negative outlook or our own. When you get tense simply remind yourself to smile again and any inner wrinkles will soon smooth over, uplifting others energy. Strengthen your inner smile by practicing it in difficult situations such as during exercise, traffic jams, long queues and when annoyed.

The bottom line: Keep the worries at bay, and practice your inner smile!

Global Leader Roles

Leaders who tend to be remembered over the course of history are probably, in most cases, those who transform organizations or, more generally, ways of thinking. The most important point for a leader in a multinational company is how the management is able to harmonize between individualism and collectivism points of view in order to achieve high productivity.

According to Muna, there are seven roles that global leaders must play:

1. Leaders have a responsibility for preparing and selecting human resources, taking care of them, and developing them.
2. Leaders must be able to work in a team, wise in delegating and empowering, and helping each other when their subordinates and colleagues are in trouble.
3. Leaders have excellent versatility as they may create the company's long-term value.
4. Leaders must know how to give direction towards goals that must be achieved.
5. Leaders must possess global mindset, have a broad point of view, be aware of cultural differences, and be able to handle different consumer preferences.
6. Leaders must have an ability to negotiate with different customers, clients, suppliers, government officials, etc.
7. Leaders must be able to handle multiple tasks and to balance work, family, and personal life. Besides, there are alternative improvements that could develop the relationship between headquarters and subsidiaries.

Do organizations follow these basic principles? It's worth evaluating the options!!

Offshore Centric Enterprises –

The offshore centric enterprise can deliver enormous economic benefits to both developed and developing nations. The integration of the work force in developing countries into global systems of production is already raising living standards, improving working conditions, and creating more jobs in those countries. Small and medium-sized businesses everywhere, particularly, are benefiting: as new services— from back-office administration to sales support—create infrastructures once only affordable to large organizations, these businesses can now participate in the global economy.

Shifting to the offshore model also presents big challenges for leaders in every sector of society. The very fact that so many more people all over the world are gaining equal access to the production process and the marketplace means much more trade and competition. Although this will create wealth and opportunity, it will also bring disruption and fear, both of which could threaten global integration. Legitimate concerns about job loss and skill shortages must be addressed in realistic and constructive ways.

The single most important challenge in shifting to offshore model—and the consideration driving most business decisions today—will be securing a supply of high-value skills. Nations and companies alike must invest in better basic educational and training programs. New kinds of managerial skills are also needed. Hierarchical, command-and-control approaches simply do not work anymore. They impede information flows inside companies, hampering the fluid and collaborative nature of work today. This is a key consideration in modern day organizations.

Global Competition in the Flat World
The cliché that the world is getting flat is dramatically true for today's organizations. With rapid advances in technology and communications, the time it takes to exert influence around the world from even the most remote locations has been reduced from years to only seconds. Business is becoming a unified global field as trade barriers fall, communication becomes faster and cheaper, and consumer tastes in everything from clothing to cellular phones converge. In the twenty first century, organizations will have to feel "at home" anywhere in the world. Companies can locate different parts of the organization wherever it makes the most business sense; top leadership in one country; technical brainpower and production in other locales.

Although this growing interdependence brings many advantages, it also means that the environment for companies is becoming extremely complex and extremely competitive. Organizations have to learn to cross lines of time, culture, and geography in order to survive. Every company, large and small, faces international competition on its home turf at the same time it confronts the need to be more competitive in international markets. Rising managers today need to know a second or third language and develop cross-cultural understanding. Large companies are working to globalize the management structures to remain competitive internationally, while even the smallest companies are searching for structures and processes that help them reap the advantages of global interdependence and minimize the disadvantages.

Organizational Turbulence

For much of the twentieth century, organizations operated in a relatively stable business environment, so managers could focus on designing structures and systems that kept the organization running smoothly and efficiently. There was little need to search for new ways to cope with increased competition or shifting customer demands. All that began to change in the 1980s, and today's organizations are struggling to catch up with the changes that have proliferated since then. Advances in computers and information technology are driving many of these changes at the same time they provide ways to cope with them. We'll see more turbulence in the days ahead. Fasten your seat belts and get ready for the ride!!

Value adding aspects of the product and/or service to the organization

There is an urgent need for Corporations to move toward value added services and away from general commodity-type services. In order to remain a leader in customer service and compete in a highly competitive market, organizations looks for ways to foster efficiencies by improving collaboration within the company and by offering value-added services that benefit its customers. "Our business is taking place at the customer's location, so what we try to do is streamline collaboration with our customers and internally with our employees," a CEO remarked. "That partnership helps us develop value-added services that can increase efficiencies for both the organizations and its customers, which makes everyone happy."

Market leaders across industries recognize services is key to driving revenue, differentiating offerings and meeting customer needs.

Cost

Increasing global competition

Mounting product price pressure

Decreasing product margins

Cycle Time

Decreasing product life cycles

Integrated customer needs

Meeting wider set of related customer needs & customer out comes

Creating new sources of differentiation

Diversifying revenue stream

Higher Margins

Longer contracts

Communication in a Global Context

To thrive in a dynamic and often stressful environment, companies must make every effort to build effective communications with those from different cultures. By recognizing and being familiar with global cultural differences, managers can become more sensitive to potential problem areas at the international, national, and business levels. Establishing organization wide communication guidelines for all individuals will go a long way in eliminating unnecessary communication problems. Such guidelines must stress the use of precise and clear language both for in-person meetings and in less personal mediums such as email. The extra time spent by organizations in communications preparation and screening as well as cultural understanding will be repaid immeasurably through improved relations not only with foreign business partners but also with all the individuals from other cultures who comprise an essential and critical part of the global business environment— the international consumer base.

Ten Ways to Improve Communications among cultures.
    Recognize that cultural differences exist between communicating parties.

Become familiar with cultural generalizations, as they may affect communications.

Try role reversal as a means to provide clues about cultural behaviors in communications.

Gather background data on communicating parties that may modify cultural generalizations.

Communicate using precise and clear statements rather than idioms or acronyms.

Consider the implications to non-native speakers when assessing the use of single language communications.

Recognize that translators limit the ability of communicators to have real-time exchanges.

Respect the different cultures as "different voices" that can be used to find common-ground agreement.

Review communications content prior to distribution to assure that information is presented without cultural or language bias.

Confirm the validity of message content at the completion of the communication

Ethical Issues in Information Technology

The term "ethics" comes from the Greek word ethike that means "character," and indeed the ancient Greeks conceived issues about what people should do in terms of impact upon character (Aristotle, 350 BCE). Nowadays, "ethics" is an inclusive term for concerns also referred to by "morality," "value," and "justice." Besides character and action, ethics in this inclusive sense is also concerned with the value or goodness of things and situations and with the justness of institutions (both formal and informal).

Much professional ethics for IT consultants, for example, revolves around preserving and developing a good reputation for being the sort of person who will regularly do good work, make sure a project is done well, and the like. One's reputation is for being the kind of person who will consistently behave well, but good character is by no means our only concern with regard to what people should do. Bad actions and bad performance can be more important than any amount of good reputation if they are bad enough. People sometime surprise us when they act "out of character." On the other hand, it is the belief in enduring character that allows people to "coast on their (good) reputations." And IT firms affirm their belief in the enduring character of technical expertise when they hire previously convicted hackers like Kevin Mitnick.

The business discipline

The business discipline under consideration is Information Technology Statement of ethical issue:

There are at least three sets of conflicting interests in Information Technology outsourcing: 1) the corporations who save large amounts of money on labor costs; 2) the offshore workers who receive better salaries in their home economies; and 3) the United States workers who lose their jobs.

Each of these parties has important considerations involving their own interests: the corporation for maximizing profits and shareholder return, the global workers for improving their income, and the U.S. workers for keeping their jobs. There are additional self- interested considerations for the corporation: Some jobs simply do not outsource well, even if the technical abilities of the workers in the two countries are the same. But even when all self-interested considerations are taken into account, there remains an ethical issue, an issue of justice. Defenders of globalization maintain that free trade of jobs will make everyone better off in the long run. This claim goes beyond considerations of self-interest and it may be true or false. Due to globalization jobs occur within a social and economic context, and it is within that context that economic inequalities are ethically justified. So why is globalization of employment any more justified than globalizing of tax liabilities?

It is clear in both cases that corporations benefit from the social and economic institutions that allow them to function in their home country. It might be expected that they make corresponding contributions to their home country even when they could do better otherwise. On an institutional level, many such principles are laws, but the ethical component of such discussion is implied in the famous statement, "There ought to be a law." The ethical question behind this statement is "Ought there to be a law?" And even if there is a law, the ethical question is "Is it a just law?" And behind this question is a major theoretical question, "What is justice?"

Identification of the business decision to be made
The range of ethical issues important for IT is perhaps broader than one might have thought. But are the issues really any different from other ethical issues? Does IT itself produce circumstances that don't fit into pre-existing ethical categories? The second question is: What features of Information

Technology create new ethical issues? There are many questions and there may not be very many answers!

Goal Setting: 5 Tips for Setting Effective New Year's Resolutions

Here are 5 tips you can use to set better New Year's resolutions.

1. Put your goal in writing. Here is how you need to think about it - if your goal is not in writing, then you do not have a goal. When we keep a goal in our heads, the goal gets crowded out by all the other pieces of information running around in our heads. Putting your goal in writing makes it real and much more likely to be accomplished. This is because you can now put your written goal somewhere that you will see it several times a day. This is a powerful reminder and keeps you on course.

2. Choose the top 1-3 of the resolutions you find both exciting & achievable in a 12 month period. Having one successful resolution is better than having 20 unsuccessful resolutions.

3. Break down the plan into small and manageable chunks. You have a full 12 months to get it done, what small things in January do you have to do to stay on track to make it to February and then to March and so on?

4. Tell lots of people about your goal. Make sure you tell one or two people that will hold you accountable to your commitment. We all need encouragement from time to time. This is because no matter how motivated we are, there are

times when we need a good swift kick in the pants. If you really want to hold your feet to the fire on this one, tell so many people about your goal that you will be embarrassed if you do not achieve it.

5. Give it all you got. Very few people have had the privilege of giving all they have toward a goal. It is a great feeling.

Global Marketing Challenges!

At the current modern stage of development the problem of strengthening the compatibility of an enterprise and its production is getting more and more urgent. Today the competitive fight is a sound step towards to the civilized market, with such notions as costumers' demands and the products themselves to be met. One of the key elements that guarantee market success is the development of the competitive product of high quality. The development of an innovation product, as I think, is one of the most risky processes, as unsound product decisions lead to huge losses.

Product decisions affect greatly on the compliance of a producer interests with those of a consumer. In general, innovation goods development covers the following problems:

- The development and introduction of new product on to the market;
- Product modification;
- Diversification of goods and their discontinued line;
- Products elimination.

Thus, for decision-making on development of the new goods carrying out of marketing researches which has specificity for the industrial enterprises is necessary. The aim of the article is mechanics of marketing researches of new product and developed algorithm of their conduction. Theoretical and methodological basis of this article is formed by the research of Ukrainian and foreign scientists in the sphere of new goods, analysis of the effectiveness of new product testing under market conditions; as well as state laws and regulations that regulate business activities in Ukraine.

There are rational approaches to the determination and analysis of marketing research to new product. The theory of innovation development was formed in the middle of the 20th century. The conceptual approach to the innovation theory was carried out by J.Schumpeter. He considered the innovation to be the change of the production technology and to have the essential meaning and importance. The modern theory of new products development is based on the results of foreign researchers of business. They underlined the importance of thorough testing of new goods concept at the early stages of the development of a new product. They considered that it is essential to make the diagnosis of goods market portfolio and only then you have to analyze new goods development strategy.

According to Schumpeter the introduction of these rules are quite natural and they are dictated by our life, as any idea never comes out from nothing: the search for the idea must be based on the accurate assessment of market demands. Thus, offered the following list of stages of a product innovation process:

1. Goods market portfolio diagnosis;
2. The strategy of new products development, generating ideas, selection and choice;
3. Economic analysis;
4. Development;
5. Testing.

But other scientists Karakai and Starostina prefer another consequence:

1. To elaborate of ideas;
2. Selection of ideas;
3. Idea development and its testing;
4. Business-analyze;
5. The analysis of possibilities of production and sale;
6. The development of a product;
7. Testing under the market conditions.

All mentioned above shows that there is no unique approach as to the development of innovating products, with the marketing approach involved. I mean the focusing on the research at the stage of generating ideas and their selection and with piloting marketing as well. In the article methods of logical results generalizing, economic and statistics methods of analysis, structural and functional analysis, as well as graphic analysis were used.

Carrying out of marketing researches has the specificity for development and deducing of the new products on the market. The concept of marketing of innovations is one of the main things of marketing activity of the enterprises policy. Paramount problem of services of marketing at the enterprises becomes carrying out of marketing researches with the purpose of revealing of a short-term level of demand and consumer motivations, presence of competing products and services and opportunities of an output of a novelty on the market. Thus there should be a communication between developers and experts in marketing for decision-making on innovative development of a product.

In the given communication it is meant an innovation not only introduction of a new product on the market, but also other innovations, such as:
1. The new or improved kinds of production (product innovations);
2. The new or improved services (innovation of services);
3. The new or improved productions and technologies (process and technological innovations);

4. The new or improved industrial systems.

Importance of marketing researches consists in the following: First, speed of occurrence of innovations has increased ability of experts in marketing to expect consumer behavior. The classical approach at which under each new idea marketing research was carried out Secondly, change in behavior of consumers. The aspiration to correspond to desires of consumers, led to occurrence of various novelties with the improved properties. Thirdly, the technology of carrying out of marketing researches leads the commercialization of production. Results of researches really give an opportunity to develop new and to modify the existing goods. Fourthly, today in market space firm's in potential of networks dominate; with existing resources of a network allow providing automatically acquaintance with the new products among a wide audience of consumers.

New products development is at the cross-roads of marketing, scientific-technical and production decisions. And the main attention is focused on costumer's needs, determination of market segments and niches in connection with technical possibilities of using achievements of science and technology to develop and promote more affective new products. The task of a new product planning consists of the search and development of alternative variants of product policy, analyzing their possible chances and risks. Within the view of improving the results of planning actions it is important to pay attention to basic problems of product innovation, which are the follows: generating ideas stage, ideas selection stage and ideas realization stage (piloting marketing).

Business Ethics!

Ethics, fairness, trust, and freedom from corruption are all part of the social capital of country, and social capital matters in financial markets because investors consider not only the available information when assessing the trade-off between risk and return but also how much they trust the accuracy of the information and the fairness of markets. The experience of WorldCom, Health-South Corporation, and Enron Corporation teaches investors that even information issued by U.S. companies cannot always be trusted, and their experience with the colluding behavior of NASDAQ's market makers and many reports of insider trading teaches them that they are not always assured of fair markets. Deficiencies in ethics and fairness mark all markets, but such deficiencies are more pronounced in some markets than in others.

Ethics and fairness in the financial markets of a company are reflected, in part, in people's assessments of the fairness of trading practices, such as insider trading. Why is insider trading considered more unfair in some countries than in others? And what can be done to improve levels of ethics and fairness around the globe? These are the questions I address in this article. I present assessments of fairness in financial trading by people in eight countries.

Culture, religion, and politics explain some differences in levels of corruption among countries. Egalitarian or individualistic religions, such as Protestantism, encourage challenges to power, whereas hierarchical religions, such as Catholicism, Eastern Orthodoxy, and Islam, discourages them. They found that Protestantism is associated with lower levels of corruption. The effect of political structure on corruption is nonlinear. Partial democratization may increase corruption, but established democracies inhibit corruption. Researchers have reported that 40 years of democracy are required for countries to become less corrupt.

Differences between ultimatum game offers in societies of vastly different standing in the global economy, such as those of the United States, the Polynesian Lamalera, and the Amazonian Machiguenga, are large. For example, although the mean offer in the ultimatum game played in Pittsburgh was 46 percent, in line with offers in other developed markets, the mean offer in the game played among the Lamalera was 56 percent; among the Machiguenga, it was only 25 percent. Some of the differences in offers to differences in market integration and differences in payoffs to cooperation. The Machiguenga, Peruvian hunter-gatherers, ranked low on ultimatum offers and also ranked low on payoffs to cooperation. The Machiguenga are almost entirely economically independent at the family level, so their well-being does not depend on cooperation with non-relatives. In contrast, the economy of the whale-hunting Lamalera depends on the cooperation of large groups of non-relatives.

In addition, there is little market integration among the Machiguenga, whose members engage in market exchange only infrequently and whose way of life would change little if markets were to disappear. In contrast, market integration among the Lamalera is substantial. Ensminger (2004) noted that the idea that people in developed market economies are more fair minded than people in societies where markets play a less prominent role seems counterintuitive because markets are often accused of undermining the moral foundations of society. But she found support for the idea in the work of earlier scholars, such as Montesquieu, who wrote in 1749 "wherever there is commerce, manners are gentle, commerce polishes and softens barbaric ways" (vol. 2, no. 8). Current levels of trust reflect past economic structures; current culture affects future economic structures. He related the prevalence of family business in Italy's Tarza region, where levels of trust are low, to its economic history of sharecropping based on long-term contracts between landowners and heads of the families who contracted on behalf of the other family members.

Leaders are change agents. Leaders should be responsible for building ethical organizations where individuals have the knowledge, skill, desire, and opportunity to personally succeed in a way that leads to collective organizational success.

Organize Your Mind to Organize Your Life!

There is a wide spread misconception that self-help books, articles, and audios are for the weak hearted. But in reality they help in changing your way of thinking which further translates into greater peace of mind, success, and happiness, provided you align and customize these ideas with your personal settings. Good things about habits are that they can be modified, reversed or sustained based on your needs. An interesting study conducted by a leading Harvard psychiatrist Dr. Paul Hammerness and leading wellness coach Margaret Moore (aka Coach Meg) on organizing your mind. In their famous book, "organize your mind to organize your life" shares the key insight; an organized mind enables full engagement in a health-giving style of life.

According to these authors:
1. The connection between disorganized minds and unhealthy habits is compelling
2. Before you can focus your attention, you must tame negative emotions
3. Exercise, deep breathing or meditation, and a good night's sleep all help mentally

While you may not think anything extra-ordinary about these findings, learning about your own strengths and weaknesses and developing positive habits based on these findings may bring in extra-ordinary results. When we think about organizing what immediately come to our mind are arranging our work place or home or removing physical clutters and using to-do lists and organizers to better control the work flow or activities. However, Dr. Hammerness and Coach Meg are moving further ahead and are sharing the views on mind's ability to attain a higher order of order -- a calm, wise, positive, strategic perspective -- and the skills it takes to get there in small or large domains of life, including health and well-being. These are based on clinical and wellness coaching experiences after working with several thousand people.

Neuroscientists are opening a window into the disorganized minds of those with attention deficit hyperactivity disorder (ADHD,) providing insights into how to train our brains to become more organized. We need to understand this is not only an issue with ADHD patients; people in all walks of life would face these challenges while trying to multi-task on variety of activities in their lives.

The connection between disorganized minds and unhealthy habits is compelling. The National Institute of Aging concluded from a recent study, as reported by CNN, that symptoms of a disorganized mind, namely impulsivity, chronic negativity, high stress and multitasking, all correlate with higher weight. For example, adults in the top 10% rating for impulsivity (most impulsive) weighed an average of 24 pounds more than those in the bottom 10% rating for impulsivity.

Organized mind depends on your ability to "drive" your attention and keep them focused. Good thing is that our brain has these powers and our job is to leverage them. Dr. Hammerness and Coach Meg recommend the following six steps in organizing your mind.

Rule No. 1: Tame your frenzy
Before you can focus your attention, you need to take charge of your negative emotional frenzy (worry, anger, sadness, irritation). This frenzy impairs and overwhelms your prefrontal cortex, the brain's CEO or executive function region, so that you can't "think straight." Too much negative stress damages your ability to focus and harms your health. The great news is that the same things that improve your health can improve your mind's ability to manage negative frenzy. Sleep well, exercise,

do a mindfulness practice or choose the slow lane from time to time, even for a few minutes. Find your unique formula to tame your frenzy so that you drive your attention to its best possible focus.

Rule No. 2: Sustain your focus
Now that your mind is calm, identify one task and one task only. The brain was not designed to focus on more than one thing at a time. Tell your brain what the intention or goal is for your focused session. Turn off your phone and e-mail, shut the door and set the timer for 20 to 30 minutes as a first step.

Rule No. 3: Apply the brakes
Your focused brain also needs to be able to stop, just as surely as a good pair of brakes brings your car to a halt at a red light. Your brain's radar regions are always scanning your internal and external environment, even when you are focused. Distractions are inevitable if you are human. Rather than mindlessly succumb to a distraction while in the midst of an important task (including health-giving activities such as exercising, cooking a healthy meal or relaxing), stop, breathe and consider whether the distraction is urgent enough to trump the current priority. If not, bring your attention back to the important task until it is

time to take a brain break to recharge your brain's batteries, or move to a new task.

Rule No. 4: Access your working memory

Your brain is designed to store a basket of bits of information in short term memory (aka "working memory"). Accessing your short-term memory, turning over various elements in your mind, helps you problem-solve, generate new ideas and insights, and see the new patterns that lead you to a strategic perspective. More great news: The same strategies that allow you to tame frenzy enable you to better access your working memory -- exercise, deep breathing or meditation, and a good night's sleep.

Rule No. 5: Shift sets

Now it's time to move your focus to a new task. Move all of your attention fully to the next task and give it your undivided attention. This brain skill, called "set-shifting," allows you to leave behind one task and leap to a new one with a fresh and productive focus. Set-shifting is also described as cognitive agility or flexibility. Often our most creative ideas come, seemingly out of the blue, when we're taking a brain break or focusing completely on something else. How interesting it is that having a fit and flexible mind is just as valuable to a life you love as a fit and flexible body.

Rule No. 6: Connect the dots

You've learned how to tame your frenzy and focus your attention on one thing at a time. You can handle distractions. Your working memory is ready for action when you need it. You are nimble, able to shift deftly from one task to the next. You take breaks, move your body and shift your focus to invite new ideas, insights and connections.

Together, these "rules of order" will help you change not only your habits of attention, but the way you look at your life. Instead of being stressed, you'll be calmly in control. You'll be more productive and therefore have more time to do things that are healthy for your body and mind. You'll feel good about yourself, and positive emotions are health promoting. And you'll be able to use your organized mind to set health and fitness goals and focus well on achieving them.

Strategic Leaders!

What successful activities or behaviors do strategic leaders engage in? To facilitate this discussion some key factors associated with strategic leadership are shared below. These are, first, those abilities to undertake organizational activity and, second, individual abilities:

Organizational ability to:
1. Be strategically orientated;
2. Translate strategy into action;
3. Align people and organizations;
4. Determine effective strategic intervention points;
5. Develop strategic competencies

Personal characteristics of:
1. A dissatisfaction or restlessness with the present;
2. Absorptive capacity;
3. Adoptive capacity
4. Leadership wisdom

Organizational abilities

a. Strategic leaders have the ability to be strategically oriented. This quality involves the ability to consider both the long-term future seeing the bigger picture, as well understanding the current contextual setting of the organization.

b. Strategic leaders have the ability to translate strategy into action. In addition to strategic leaders leading the creation of an appropriate strategy for the organization is the need to translate strategy into action by converting it into operational terms.
c. Strategic leaders have the ability to align people and organizations. This ability involves aligning individuals, or the school as a whole, to a future organizational state or position.
d. Strategic leaders have the ability to determine effective intervention points. Strategic leaders are able to define the key moment for strategic change in organizations. Strategic leadership does indeed matter. It seems the real question is not whether it matters but rather under what conditions, when, how and on what criteria.

e. Strategic leaders have the ability to develop strategic capabilities. Leadership thinkers Prahalad and Hamel use the term 'core competencies' while researcher Stalk use the term 'strategic capabilities'. Either way, the key message is to ability of leaders to develop core capabilities that differentiates them.

Personal characteristics

1. Strategic leaders have a dissatisfaction or restlessness with the present. This restlessness involves what researcher Senge describes as 'creative tension' which emerges from seeing clearly where one wishes to be, one's vision, and facing the truth about one's current reality.
2. Strategic leaders have absorptive capacity. They have the ability to absorb new information and assimilate it and learn from it and importantly to apply it to new ends.
3. Strategic leaders have adaptive capacity. They have the ability to change which is termed as 'adaptive capacity'.
4. Strategic leaders have leadership wisdom. Wisdom may simply be defined as the capacity to take the right action at the right time.

Finally, if moral leadership is to be exercised and pedagogy re-engineered with any degree of success, then future strategic leaders will need a firm set of personal values. No doubt many will have their own lists, but integrity, social justice, humanity, respect, loyalty and a sharp distinction between right and wrong, will all need to be included. Strategic relationships will soon flounder unless such a value system is held with conviction and exercised on a regular consistent basis.

Creating High Performance Organizational Culture

Organizations are the most important aspect of modern day's human society but they have not received the desired attention that deserved. Organizational Behavior is the study and application of knowledge about how people, individuals, and groups act in organizations. It does this by taking a system approach. That is, it interprets people-organization relationships in terms of the whole person, whole group, whole organization, and whole social system. Its purpose is to build better relationships by achieving human objectives, organizational objectives, and social objectives. The behavior of organizations constantly undergoes changes with business trends and evolving global strategies. To succeed in increasingly competitive domestic and global markets, organizations must create and motivate a workforce that is able to realize competitive advantage.

What type of performance is necessary to attain such an advantage is heavily dependent on the market a firm is in and the strategic choices a firm makes. Firms that operate in markets where, for example, price is the dominant performance indicator likely will opt for producing large quantities of a limited set of products or services. Standardization and repetition of work processes will contribute to high levels of efficiency, and, thus add to competitive value. Manufacturing organizations fall into this category. Facilitating outstanding routine performance requires an appropriate management of human resources by creating structures, rules and procedures so that work across individual employees and groups can be coordinated and controlled in effective and efficient ways according to Human Resource Management.

If innovation and being innovative are prime performance indicators an organization may prefer a strategy to offer customer made products that fulfill the unique needs of individual clients. This will lead to work processes that are primarily non-routine in nature and demand creative workers. Such a firm needs a HRM (Human Resource Management) policy that stimulates employees to engage in creative and innovative courses of actions that may substantially deviate from fixed patterns of work behavior. The HRM policies should focus on interpersonal relations, interdependencies and processes such as trust, learning, communication, and information exchange between employees. IT Services and Consulting organizations fall into the innovative category. The organization's base rests on management's philosophy, values, vision and goals. This in turn drives the organizational culture which is composed of the formal organization, informal organization, and the social environment. The culture determines the type of leadership, communication, and group dynamics within the organization. The workers perceive this as the quality of work life which directs their degree of motivation. The final outcome is performance, individual satisfaction, and personal growth and development. All these elements combine to build the model or framework that the organization operates from.

Four major models or frameworks that typical organizations operate are:

1. Autocratic - The basis of this model is power with a managerial orientation of authority. The employees in turn are oriented towards obedience and dependence on the boss. The employee need that is met is subsistence. The performance result is minimal.
2. Custodial - The basis of this model is economic resources with a managerial orientation of money. The employees in turn are oriented towards security and benefits and

dependence on the organization. The employee need that is met is security. The performance result is passive cooperation.

3. Supportive - The basis of this model is leadership with a managerial orientation of support. The employees in turn are oriented towards job performance and participation. The employee need that is met is status and recognition. The performance result is awakened drives.

4. Collegial - The basis of this model is partnership with a managerial orientation of teamwork. The employees in turn are oriented towards responsible behavior and self-discipline. The employee need that is met is self-actualization. The performance result is moderate enthusiasm.

Although there are four separate models, almost no organization operates exclusively in one. There will usually be a predominate one, with one or more areas over-lapping in the other models. The first model, autocratic, had its roots in the industrial revolution. The managers of this type of organization operate out of McGregor's Theory X. The next three models begin to build on McGregor's Theory Y. They have each evolved over a period of time and there is no one "best" model. The collegial model should not be thought as the last or best model, but the beginning of a new model or paradigm.

Finally, creating a high performing and innovative organization also requires cooperation among employees who differ in their knowledge, skills, and abilities. Cooperation implies knowledge sharing, finding solutions together, learning from one another and realizing synergy in creative and innovative processes.

Critical Thinking Approach to Ethical Leadership Decision Making

Success in the modern business firm requires the development of critical thinking skills: the ability to understand what someone is saying and then to apply evaluative criteria to assess the quality of the reasoning offered to support the conclusion. There are many forms of critical thinking, but they all share one characteristic: They focus on the quality of someone's reasoning. Critical thinking is active; it challenges each of us to form judgments about the quality of the link between someone's reasons and conclusions. This article review ethical theories and applies these theories with critical thinking approach for ethical leadership decision making.

Business Ethics and Leadership

How does one link between Critical thinking, business ethics, and leadership? American Heritage Dictionary defines ethics as the moral quality of a course of action; any set of moral principles or values; the study of the general nature of morals and of the specific moral choices to be made by the individual in his [or her] relationship with others. Business ethics is a subset of the study of ethics and is defined as the study of what makes up good and bad business conduct. This conduct occurs when the firm acts as an organization, as well as when individual managers make decisions inside the organization.

Examining what comprises the organizational culture should reveal some key attributes that encourage ethical behavior. Scholars who studied organizational reputation maintained that a positive reputation, such as one for ethical behavior, had a beneficial effect in the marketplace. The sum total of individual employees' ethical values influences corporate conduct, especially in a corporation's early years. The activities during these years, in turn, form the basis of what constitutes a corporate culture, or an environment for doing business. In a free-market society, values of productivity, efficiency, and profits become part of the culture of all companies.
Theories of ethical thought

Consequential theories
Ethicists, businesspeople, and workers who adhere to a consequential theory of ethics judge acts as ethically good or bad based on whether the acts have achieved their desired results. The actions of a business or any other societal unit are looked at as right or wrong only in terms of whether the results

can be rationalized. This theory is best exemplified by the utilitarian school of thought, which is divided into two sub-schools: act utilitarianism and rule utilitarianism. In general, adherents of this school judge all conduct of individuals or businesses on whether it brings net happiness or pleasure to a society. They judge an act ethically correct after adding up the risks (unhappiness) and the benefits (happiness) to society and obtaining a net outcome.

Deontological theories

Deontology is derived from a Greek word meaning "duty." For advocates of deontology, rules and principles determine whether actions are ethically good or bad. The consequences of individual actions are not considered. The Golden Rule, "Do unto others as you would have them do unto you," is the hallmark of the theory. Absolute deontology claims that actions can be judged ethically good or bad on the basis of absolute moral principles arrived at by human reason regardless of the consequences of an action; that is, regardless of whether there is net happiness. Immanuel Kant provided an example of an absolute moral principle in his widely studied "categorical imperative." He stated that a person ought to engage only in acts that he or she could see becoming a universal standard.

Humanist theories

A third school of thought, the humanist school, evaluates actions as ethically good or bad depending on what they contribute to improving inherent human capacities such as intelligence, wisdom, and self-restraint.

Profit-oriented theory

The profit-oriented theory of social responsibility begins with a market-oriented concept of the firm that most readers were exposed to in their first or second course in economics. Holders of this theory argue that business entities are distinct organizations in our society and that their sole purpose is to increase profits for shareholders. Businesses are to be judged solely on criteria of economic efficiency and how well they contribute to growth in productivity and technology. Corporate social responsibility is shown by managers who maximize profits for their shareholders, who, in turn, are able to reinvest such profits, providing for increased productivity, new employment opportunities, and increased consumption of goods.

Managerial theory

Advocates of the managerial theory of social responsibility argue that businesses, particularly large institutions, have a number of interest groups or constituents both internally and externally that they must deal with regularly, not just stockholders and a board of directors. A business has employees, customers, suppliers, consumers, activist groups, government regulators, and others that influence decision making and the ability of the entity to make profits.

Conclusions

It is whether or not we foster the development of wisdom--through Business Ethics--that will ultimately dictate the direction in which our part of the universe moves. In fact, the idea that human beings are acting as co-creators for the present and future is something that has become a tangible reality. When examining business ethics, one must recognize that the corporations, partnerships, and other entities that make up the business community are a composite of individuals. Corporations, and the culture of a corporation, are greatly influenced by what ethical values individuals bring to them. For an organization as a whole to be ethical, it must have an organizational culture that values ethical decision-making. The best way to achieve the ethical value in organization is to foster critical thinking in organizations.

Organizational Behavior: The Paradigm Shift

"In a few hundred years, when the history of our time will be written from a long-term perspective, it is likely that the most important event historians will see is not technology, not the Internet, not e-commerce. It is an unprecedented change in the human condition. For the first time - literally - substantial and rapidly growing numbers of people have choices. For the first time, they will have to manage themselves. And society is totally unprepared for it."

--Peter F. Drucker

A prelude to organizational behavior study

Traditional management education focuses on competency such as accounting, finance, marketing, operations and information technology related areas. However, with the growth and expansion of organizational needs, it has become essential to understand the process of management to be successful in the competitive global market place. Within this process view of management now the attention is given to the roles, behaviors, and skills that are necessary for effective managerial performance. Some of these behavioral 'soft' skills are communicating with peers, subordinates, and bosses; obtaining and sharing information; running meetings; allocating resources to different groups; and handling conflict within or between teams.

The understanding of management processes, often referred to as organizational behavior (OB) extends managerial education to the study of people, groups, and their interactions in organizations. Changing business environment demands broader skill sets that helps in problem solving, decision-making, and handling communication and interpersonal relationships.

Historical background of organizational development
Essence of leadership was first recorded by the Greek philosopher Plato. Aristotle introduced persuasive communication in leadership. Niccolò Machiavelli in 16th century laid the foundation for organizational power and politics. Adam Smith in 1776 brought in organizational structure based-on division of labor. In late 18th century, German sociologist Max Weber introduced the idea of rational organizations. Weber also initiated discussion of charismatic leadership. Soon after, systematic goal setting, and reward was introduced by Frederick Winslow Taylor. Elton Mayo and his

colleagues in 1920's have done productivity studies in Hawthorne laboratory.

Schools of historical thought on organizational theory

Studies show systematic transformation of the orientation from machine into human potential. In general, while examining the history of organizational behavior, a marked shift from scientific management era to more human behavior approach in organizations is evident. The basic assumptions underlying human behavior were now perceived to be oriented to personal growth, accomplishment, and inner development. If managers were to become truly effective, it was argued, they must go beyond simply providing fair pay and treatment and attempt to make organizational members feel important.

Understanding an organization

An organization is a tool used by people to coordinate actions to obtain something desire or value—that is, to achieve their goals. The production of goods and services most often takes place in an organizational setting because people working together to produce goods and services usually can create more value than people working separately. Organizations exist because of their ability to create value and acceptable outcomes for various groups of stakeholders, people who have an interest, claim, or stake in the organization, in what it does, and in how well it performs. Most people have a casual attitude toward organizations because organizations are intangible. Today, many organizations being founded, and particularly those experiencing the fastest growth, are producing goods and services related in some way to new information technology. The increasing use of computers and new information technologies such as the Internet are revolutionizing the way all organizations operate.

Organizational theory is the study of how organizations function and how they affect and are affected by the environment in which they operate. For any organization, an appropriate structure to facilitates effective responses to problems of coordination and motivation—problems that can arise for any number of environmental, technological, or human reasons that need to be addressed. As organizations grow and differentiate, the structure likewise evolves. Organizational structure and culture are the means the organization uses to achieve its goals; organizational design is about how and why various means are chosen. Further, organizational structure can be managed through the process of organizational design and change.
Global Dimensions of Organizational Behavior

In the globalization age corporate success is increasingly linked to worldwide operations and a global staff. Top executive teams have learned first-hand one of the foremost lessons of doing business in international markets to understand the local culture. All around the globe, people working in large and small businesses alike are facing the many challenges and opportunities associated with business competition in an increasingly complex and "borderless" world. The ability to respect differences and value diversity is an important key to success in managing organizational behavior across cultures.

Summary and conclusions

Today's organizations need managers with global awareness and cultural sensitivity. This does not mean that they all must work in foreign lands. But it does mean that they must be aware of how international events may affect the well-being of organizations. They must know how to deal with people from other countries and cultures. Especially for those who cross cultural and national boundaries, understanding these differences is critical for success working in an interconnected world.

Today, managers must be inquisitive and willing to learn quickly from management practices around the globe. Insights into effective management and high performance organizations are not restricted to any one location or culture. Contributions to our understanding about people and organizations can be found from Africa to Asia and from Europe to North and South America. Finally, in the interest of effective and efficient organizational performance, managers should create jobs and organizational structures that allowed people an opportunity to develop their abilities and to experience personal growth.

The Power of Habit!

"We are what we repeatedly do. Excellence, therefore, is not an act but a habit." - Aristotle

Here is an interesting story about a woman named Lisa Allen, reported by Charles Duhigg, in his recent book, The Power of Habit. Lisa started smoking and drinking from the age of sixteen and by that time she reached thirty, she was obese, troubled with deeper debt, and with unstable jobs. Here is another status of the same women, in the next phase of her life; lean and vibrant with toned legs of a runner. She firmly established in her job, she is debt free and not touched a drink or smoked for over four years. She lost sixty pounds and ran a marathon since then. She was an interesting study for neurologist, psychologists, geneticists, and sociologists. The researchers' goal was to identify how habits work at the neurological level – and what it took them to change.

How changes do happen in behaviors? What is causing the transformation? Research findings are very interesting. By focusing on one pattern – what is known as "key stone habit" –

one can reprogram other routines as well. In the above mentioned study, Lisa changed her smoking habit which created a chain reaction that lead to change in other habits as well. In a larger context, business organizations get transformed by changing habits, starting with a single key activity change.

William James (1842 –1910) a pioneering American psychologist and philosopher wrote in 1892, "All our life, so far as it has definite form, is but a mass of habits". Most decisions we make day to day may feel like well thought over actions, but they are not. They are habits. One of the studies by Duke University in 2006 found that 40 percent of decisions people performed were not actual decisions, but habits. High performing athletes and other high achievers build their skills but routine practice which eventually become part of their DNA, or their daily habit.

To a greater extent, our habits define our destiny. Although each habit may look little on its own, over time, the way we deal with our day to day activities including what we eat, whom we talk to, how we deal with children, how we deal with money, how often we exercise have enormous impact on our health, wealth, and happiness. Have you ever noticed your own driving habits? There are no special thoughts on your actions at every stage of your driving. If you closely observe you follow a particular patterns based on the habits you developed.

Habits never really disappear. They are encoded into the structure of our brain and that is a huge advantage for us, because it could be awful, if we need to relearn to drive after every vacation. The problem is that your brain cannot tell which is a good habit or a bad habit. So, if you have a bad habit, it is lurking there, waiting for the right cue or rewards. Habits are powerful, but delicate. They can be deliberately designed or can emerge outside our consciousness. They often occur without our permission. They shape our lives far more than we realize. They are so strong that they cause our brains to cling to them, exclusion of all else, including common sense.

The central argument of this article can be very exciting to all. Habits can be changed, if we understand how they work. We need to make conscious choice of what we want to accomplish. To drink or to run is a choice one has to make deliberately. Repeat the process till it becomes a habit. Then stop making the choice and the neuron in our brain will ensure we follow the pattern and the behavior will become automatic.

Let me also share some very basic tips that work for you. Many behavioral scientists have reported that if you repeat an activity at least 21 days without break it may help in habit formation. So, chose one good activity and practice it to become a "keystone habit" and then sustain it. Always remember that you have a higher purpose in life and choosing the right habits will take you to the destination you wanted to go!

The Success Code!

If you want to become a winner you were born to be, it is going to take changing your daily actions until they become a habit. The fact that you created a vision and understand the true value and purpose of that vision will energize you and give you personal motivation you need to finish well- and achieve exceptional results. Mahatma Gandhi, who led India's independence, was an average person with limited success in his early career. Some life changing experiences he had in South Africa as a young attorney discovered his "purpose in life" which motivated him to "persist without exception". With that vision and purpose he led the entire nation to independence without firing a shot!

Much about success is just the result if simply the ability to follow up, follow through, and finish what you started. You are not beaten by being knocked down. You're only beaten if you stay down. You are what you are and where you are because of what's gone into your mind, but you can change what you are and where you are by changing what goes into your mind. Choices determine that action you take, and action produces the results of your life. You can only think in ways consistent with the information you have in your mind. So to change what you do, you have to change the way you think, and to think differently, you need to change what goes into your mind. There are six characteristics that comprise the foundation stones of your life and success. They are: honesty, character, faith, integrity, love, and loyalty. These six foundational stones essentially provide the raw material for your thinking. As such, they become the core characteristics of what you be, do, and have, which ultimately determines the results you get in life. These stones form the code for success or failure because you are thinking and your actions must be consistent with the characteristics of the foundation you build. The idea of value and purpose is linked to the concept of discovering a great good, a mission, or higher calling. This is applicable at individual and at business level. High performing individuals and organizations have discovered this higher calling. Fundamentally, we need to understand one universal principle: You can have everything in life you want if you will just help enough other people get what they want. This is another-centered strategy; not self-centered.

Finally, to have success, one must develop the following three dimensions of life. The first dimension is spiritual, the second dimension is mental, and the third dimension is physical. Each dimension is separate, but they work together to create a total person. The most important and the most neglected dimension is spiritual. It is out of our souls our attitude flows, and our attitude defines our altitude in life. The depth of our spirit will determine the height of our success.

Our mental abilities are housed in our brains, and if you think our brain as a muscle, you need the importance of exercising it daily to keep it in top condition. The best exercise for brain and your mind is to force it to think which is enabled by continuous learning and education. Taking care of physical condition and health is very essential for our overall success. We need to have good eating and wait control plans and regular exercise. If we want to provide our spirit and mind a top notch house to live-in we need to keep our body in excellent shape.

Our success greatly depends on how we align these three dimensions, viz; spiritual, mental, physical. This is my personal testimony. I believed in all three dimensions from very early age in my life, but my priorities were in different order. Some life changing experiences gave me deeper insight which helped me reprioritize the dimensions to the right order: i.e., spiritual, mental, and physical. This change in priority clearly brought greater success and happiness in my life.

Words and Destiny!

"The words you consistently select will shape your destiny" - Anthony Robbins, motivational speaker and leadership coach. Your words have incredible power. They can make or break you; they can help you build a bright future, destroy your opportunities, or maintain the status quo. You may wonder how such bold statement can be made. Your words reinforce your beliefs... and your beliefs create your reality. Let me share the logical reasoning and how the process flow works.

Thoughts >> Words>>Beliefs>>Actions>> Results

Every end result begins with a thought, positive or negative. Let's assume someone have a thought that he is not good at his work. He maintain such thoughts on a regular basis may be hundreds of thousands of times in his life. He starts words that support such thoughts to his friends and colleagues. Here again he repeat these self-talk again and again thereby reinforcing the beliefs. These beliefs get strengthened over a period of time and get embedded in his subconscious mind. What this lead to be taking little or no action in his work area to improve, since he has already resigned to fate based on the belief which is embedded in the mind. To make things worse, he will have more negative words on his activities, reinforcing negative beliefs and getting more negative results. It is a vicious cycle! The whole situation would have reversed if he started with the right thoughts, which then lead to right beliefs and actions which will end up with right results.

Rudyard Kipling has famously stated, "words are, of course, the most powerful drug used by mankind". Don't underestimate the role of words in our destiny. You can't keep repeating the negative words and expect to be high achiever, whereas positive language moves you towards your goal. According to Plutarch, "in words are seen the state of mind, character, and disposition of the speaker". What obstacles you are facing in your life right now? Imagine the power you could unleash if you saw them as "just barely an inconvenience" instead of an insurmountable barrier.

Words and accountability: When it comes to personal and business relationships avoid "burning the bridges", but sometimes the only way to move forward in life – and to achieve an ambitious goal – is cut off from the negative people. Always discuss your plans with people who can render an intelligent opinion on the subject.

Words and emotions: Our vocabulary affects our emotions, our beliefs, and our effectiveness in life. Aggressive words like "furious", "livid", "enraged" etc. would infuriate you and add more blood pressure and change in your physiology. Replace them with lighter words like, "annoyed", "peeved" etc. which would break the negative emotions completely. In a positive sense, instead of saying "I'm determined", why not say, "I'm unstoppable" and instead of saying "I'm OK, try "I'm phenomenal" or "I feel just tremendous". Always choose words that will point you in the direction of your goals.

Fortunately, you can control your words – which means that you have the ability to build a positive belief system and produce the results you want. Remember, it's up to you to speak in a way that will toward what you want in life. Therefore, use words that are consistent with the path you truly wish to be on take action along the lines and watch yourself begin to travel in that wonderful direction!

Risk Management Strategies in the Global Environment

"Nothing splendid has ever been achieved except those who dared believe that something inside of them was superior to circumstance." – Bruce Barton

Today more than ever before, business professionals and leaders are challenged with increasingly difficult and diverse responsibilities, including understanding and employing decisions based on intense and complex business theories. Leaders also face a myriad of internal and external factors driving success or failure in enterprise business. In the age of dynamics and diverse global business enterprise, business professionals need to expand their existing base of knowledge related to various risk management strategies to be successful in the marketplace. Risk management process involves assessing, or evaluating risk and developing management strategies to mitigate them. These strategies include risk transfer, risk avoidance, and accepting some or all the risk. Financial risk management strategies focus on risk managed through financial instruments.

To achieve sustainable competitive advantage, the organizations have to be creative with innovation and adaptable to dynamic risk management strategies. Today more than ever, the premium comes from the fusion of invention and insight into how to transform how things are done. In addition, the spread of shared technologies and business standards is creating an unprecedented opportunity for global integration, not just within each sector of society, but across them all. As the boundaries between the traditional "estates" become more porous, new businesses can contribute new forms of commerce, learning, and good governance. One of the way to handle the risk is to integrate the business in a global level.

Globally Integrated Enterprise Approach

The globally integrated enterprise will require fundamentally different approaches to production, distribution, and work-force deployment. Apart from off- loading non-core activities, the efforts are used for integrating the organization in multiple ways among suppliers, and customers.

Opportunities and risks

The globally integrated enterprise can deliver enormous economic benefits to both developed and developing nations. The integration of the workforce in developing countries into global systems of production is already raising living standards, improving working conditions, and creating more jobs in those countries. Small and medium-sized businesses everywhere, particularly, are benefiting: as new services— from back-office administration to sales support—create infrastructures once only affordable to large organizations, these businesses can now participate in the global economy.

Shifting to the model of globally integrated enterprises also presents big challenges for leaders in every sector of society. The very fact that so many more people all over the world are gaining equal access to the production process and the marketplace means much more trade and competition. Although this will create wealth and opportunity, it will also bring disruption and fear, both of which could threaten global integration. Legitimate concerns about job loss and skill shortages must be addressed in realistic and constructive ways.

The single most important challenge in shifting to globally integrated enterprises—and the consideration driving most business decisions today—will be securing a supply of high-value skills. Nations and companies alike must invest in better basic educational and training programs. New kinds of managerial skills are also needed. Hierarchical, command-and-control approaches simply do not work anymore. They impede information flows inside companies, hampering the fluid and collaborative nature of work today. This is a key consideration in modern day organizations.

Globally integrated organizations are seen as the next generation which optimizes operations and reduce cost by cutting down non-revenue generating expenses and reduce risk in a global context. Early adapters of this approach like IBM have proved the efficacy of this model.

Conclusion

Success of any organization depends on organizational leaders. So this discussion brings in challenging questions to board members and senior executive leadership. Are they looking for only short-term financial results or long-term organizational results by handling global risk effectively? In a fast-changing world, organizations are looking for transformational leaders who have the vision to translate the organizations into high performing cultures in a globally integrated enterprise. This is a challenging task worth emulating.

Some leadership thoughts in troubled times!

I am a student on leadership studies and also a practicing leader with varying degree of success. There are umpteen numbers of definitions on leadership. My intent is not to define leadership, but share some views on how leadership shapes up individuals and organizations.

Turbulent times build great leaders. Hard conditions reveal a person. Crises contain exceptional opportunity. The best leaders are the product of most uncomfortable conditions. We have numerous stories to share on this count from the early days of recorded history.

Average mortals avoid confrontations and in the process miss the glorious chance of our buried potential. Doing nothing in turbulent times is the worst one can do. Failures make us afraid to take bold steps. In a professional / leadership setting, resisting what make you feel uncomfortable at work and playing safe at wild times seems to be a safe bet, but in long term it's a very dangerous maneuver. A great skier achieves his greatness by trying at super-hard terrains regularly. There is no bigger truth than this; when you go to your limits, your limits will expand. The more time you spend outside your comfort zone, the wider it grows. True leaders eat their fear before the fear eats them.

In an organizational setting, deficiencies get amplified in turbulent conditions. The recent economic conditions really tested many individuals and business organizations. While several organizations got folded up, the smart and agile ones excelled and even grew at a faster pace than the industry standards. In reality, intelligent enterprises got free consulting advice during these stress tests. The key takeaway from our recent experience is that the organizations must learn to become comfortable with discomfort.

How can someone become dramatically more effective? In a leadership and personally development context, this is what I would recommend. Take bold steps. The very things that make you afraid are the doorways into your leadership best. Our natural tendency is to hang on to the safe harbor of the known. Then we'll never conquer new land or reach the summit.

Setbacks are nothing more than tests to see if you are ready for rewards that are available to you. Most people give up while seeing a wall. You please don't.

Please remember; if you have not failed, you have not tried enough. You can't get a break through without going through a period of breakdown. Change is always messiest in the middle. Everything in your past, including the hard times and bitterness you experienced, was necessary preparation to bring you to the edge where you are finally ready to make the true leader you are capable of. Looking silly feels uncomfortable for a minute, but letting your doubts and fears own you feel uncomfortable for a life time.

Let me close this article with a statement from the legendary world cycling champion, Lance Armstrong, who faced several adversities. Armstrong said, "pain is temporary; quitting lasts forever." He fought hard the cancer pain and made a huge comeback to life and to his beloved spot of cycling and never gave up. Great leaders and organizations never quit. They are not afraid of failures or initial setbacks. So in this troubled economic times, let's keep our focus on the goals for the better future for all.

Positive Intelligence: A Game Changer

Your potential is determined by many factors, including your cognitive intelligence (IQ), your emotional intelligence (EQ), and your skills, knowledge, experience, and social network. But it is your Positive Intelligence (PQ) that determines what percentage of your vast potential you actually achieve. When your mind is on your side, you flourish; when your mind works against you, you flounder. People who cultivate a positive mind-set perform better in the face of challenge.

Shirzad Chamine, Executive Coach and NY Times Bestselling Author of 'Positive Intelligence', shares compelling reasons for focusing on, measuring, and improving your Positive Intelligence. Positive Intelligence is ultimately about action and results. Its tools and techniques are a synthesis of the best practices in neuroscience, organizational science, positive psychology, and Co-Active® coaching.

With Positive Intelligence you can significantly improve the percentage of time that your mind is acting as your friend, rather than as your enemy. This will permanently shift the balance of power inside your mind so you can achieve more of your vastly untapped potential and help others do the same.

Research Evidence

Current breakthrough research in neuroscience, organizational science, and positive psychology validates the principles of Positive Intelligence and the relationship between higher PQ and both performance and happiness. As mentioned, PQ measures the percentage of time that your brain is working positively, in your best interest, versus negatively, in self-sabotage. Though different researchers have used different methods to track positivity and calculate positive-to-negative ratios, the results have been remarkably consistent.

Here are some of the research results reported by Shirzad Chamine in his book 'Positive Intelligence'. An analysis of more than two hundred different scientific studies, which collectively tested more than 275,000 people, concluded that higher PQ leads to higher salary and greater success in the arenas of work, marriage, health, sociability, friendship, and creativity.

1. Salespeople with higher PQ sell 37 percent more than their lower- PQ counterparts.

2. Negotiators with higher PQ are more likely to gain concessions, close deals, and forge important future business relationships as part of the contracts they negotiate.
3. Higher-PQ workers take fewer sick days and are less likely to become burned out or quit.
4. Doctors shifted to higher PQ make accurate diagnoses 19 percent faster.
5. Students shifted to higher PQ perform significantly better on math tests.
6. Higher-PQ CEOs are more likely to lead happy teams who report their work climate to be conducive to high performance. Project teams with higher- PQ managers perform 31 percent better on average when other factors are held equal.
7. Managers with higher PQ are more accurate and careful in making decisions, and they reduce the effort needed to get their work done.
8. A comparison of sixty teams showed that a team's PQ was the greatest predictor of its achievement.

Besides impacting both performance and happiness, higher PQ can also literally impact your health and longevity:

1. Research has shown that higher PQ results in enhanced immune system functioning, lower levels of stress-related hormones, lower blood pressure, less pain, fewer colds,

better sleep, and less likelihood to have hypertension, diabetes, or strokes.
2. And, most amazingly, Catholic nuns whose personal journals in their early twenties showed higher PQ lived nearly ten years longer than the other nuns in their group. Higher PQ can literally help you live longer.
3. 75 IS A CRITICAL TIPPING POINT

If your PQ score is 75 or higher, then your mind is on your side, and it can help you spiral up. Shirzad writes: "… the PQ score of 75 is a critical tipping point. Above it, you are generally being uplifted by the internal dynamics of the mind, and below it you are constantly being dragged down by those dynamics."

To measure your PQ, you can do so at www.PositiveIntelligence.com/Assessments.
A high measurement of the PQ score is not a bad sign at all. It is a wakeup call to realize where you stand and what action you need to take.

The First Person You Must Lead is YOU

The smallest crowd you will ever lead is you—but it's the most important one. If you do that well, then you will earn the right to lead even bigger crowds. Leading yourself well means that you hold yourself to a higher standard of accountability than others do. Leadership is a trust, not a right. For that reason, you must "fix" yourself earlier than others may be required to.

Dr. John C Maxwell, world famous speaker and bestselling author stated, "to lead others, first lead yourself". Learning to lead yourself well is one of the most important things you'll ever do as a leader. Most people use two totally different sets of criteria for judging themselves and judging others. We tend to judge others according to their actions. It's very cut-and-dried. However, we judge ourselves by our intentions. Even if we do the wrong thing, we let ourselves off the hook if we believe our intentions are good. That's part of the reason we allow ourselves to make the same mistakes over and over again before we are willing to make real changes.

Retired Brig. Gen. Rebecca Halstead, the first female West Point graduate to be promoted to general of US Army says,

"The first person you lead is yourself. If you have to remind people that you are the leader, you're not." According to Gen Halstead, leaders need to train their brains to do difficult things, such as getting up to go running when they would rather sleep. They need to be physically, spiritually, emotionally and mentally fit to think forward.

Thomas J. Watson, the former chairman of IBM, said, "Nothing so conclusively proves a man's ability to lead others as what he does from day to day to lead himself." Leaders receive very little fanfare for quietly leading themselves well day in and day out. Most people are unaware of the disciplines their leaders practice or the sacrifices they make outside of the spotlight. However, they don't do it for recognition; they do it for results. What leaders do day-to-day always pays off in the long run. Success or failure isn't an event, but a process.

New Year – Yes, You Can!!

Here are few tips on how to make your New Year resolution stick.

1. On the work front, work smart with plans and priorities which will yield better results than shear hard work. Surround yourself with smart, motivated and dynamic people who could compliment you in your efforts. Stay away from emotional vampires and learned to say 'no' when required. Developing healthy habits and balancing is key; make sure you find sufficient time for sleep, exercise, eating well and taking care of yourself. Plan your leisure time and vacations in advance similar to business schedules which you plan well in advance. Don't burn the candle on both ends, say 'no' to unplanned activities, if possible.

2. On the health front, have quantifiable and measurable goals. For example, commit to lose certain amount of weight within a specific period, keep your vitals within the specific margins, or participate in specific sporting events and achieve the desired performance levels within the specified timeframe. As you know, the motivation does not last long unless you practice daily. Reward good behavior and punish bad choices. Compete with

yourself, don't compare with someone else, particularly when it comes to fitness goals.

3. On the spiritual front, try to connect with the higher being. Prayer and meditation would bring joy and happiness and will reduce stress significantly. We are here in this earth for a purpose. Know your calling.

My Marathon Story

I have joined an elite club of Marathoners on Sunday, January 19, 2014 at the age of 50, covering official distance of 42.195 kilometers (26 miles and 385 yards) in a road race at PF Chang's Rock 'n' Roll Arizona Marathon. Prior to this first full marathon attempt, my best running records were a successful completion of half marathon in 2013 and an unofficial run of 16 miles few weeks prior to the current marathon.

I am sharing this story with just one objective. If I can do it, anyone else can do it. I am not particularly athletic. In fact, I was impacted by arthritis several years ago and had even difficulty in walking. I was under medication for several years. One fine day I threw my medicine chest out and developed some discipline and mental toughness over a period of time to achieve this goal.

Life lessons of marathon: Unlike a sprint track which is often straight, a marathoner's track may typically have twist and turns. As a consequence, the runner has to make constant adjustments for speed depending on the terrain, decide on when to take a break, when to sip that water, and when to catch his breath. If we draw parallels, life is like a long distance runner with constant course correction; it's all about strategy and persistence. Unlike a sprinter, in a marathon, you are not competing with someone; you are competing with yourself. Someone overtaking does not bother you. You run your race with patience, confidence in the game-plan, and steadiness of your pace, knowing and trusting your stamina, ability and timing, sure that you will catch up sooner or later with those who went on ahead.

Back to my story: Today, for me, running is a spiritual experience. When I run I transcend space and time. To me life is a marathon, not a sprint. For the many projects that I have undertaken in my workplace, spiritual organizations and in my family, I learned that what finally matters is the inner strength to finish the task at hand. Continued persistence that matters; to be able to draw deep and pull something out of yourself is one of the most tremendous things that you learn out of your marathon experience.

Honestly, I was very ill prepared for the run; a week before I was down with flu and was bed ridden. I could barely move. My situation was not good even a day before my run. It was a battle between mind and body and my mind prevailed over my body.

My wife knew that I would do it, irrespective of whatever odds I may face. My daughter knew why I wanted to do it. And, outwardly the most courageous man, my son, was really scared of my health and wellbeing and pleaded me not to go for it. I promised him that I won't do any harm for myself. He is happy and relieved now. I continued to run marathons ever since and there is no turning back.

I dedicated my first marathon run for my beloved daughter to fulfill her dreams. And, she did it!!

Five Universal Citizens

Five Universal Citizens - Their actions transcend the geographical boundaries.

1. Dr. Kalam, a saintly scientist who rekindled the imagination of Indians, rose from humble origins to become the President of India. This 'People's President', as he affectionately called, was beyond caste, creed and political boundaries. This 'modern day Gandhi' was widely respected by the common men and intellectuals alike. In his passing on Jul 27, 2015, the world has lost a true leader who inspired generations through his pioneer services in science, technology, writings, teachings and visionary leadership.

2. Pope Francis, first Jesuit priest to become a Pope, affectionately called the common man's Pope is reshaping the Catholic Church and also giving new directions on how to make the planet a better place to live. Pope Francis is well known for his humility, concern for the poor and also his commitment to interfaith dialogue.

3. Patriarch Aphrem II, leader of the ancient Orthodox Syriac Christian Church, came to lead the Church at a

very difficult time in the Church history. He took over from a saintly predecessor and in no time has shown his ability as a worthy successor by fearlessly staying with the oppressed and raising the awareness of persecution people in the Middle East where Christianity was originated. He is also working hard for church unity and universal brotherhood.

4. The 14th Dalai Lama, arguably the wisest man living in this planet today, is well known for his discourses on wide ranging topics. His focus is on the promotion of basic human values or secular ethics in the interest of human happiness, the fostering of inter-religious harmony and the preservation of Tibet's Buddhist culture, a culture of peace and non-violence.

5. The most controversial and potentially the most powerful among the list is President Obama, leader of the most powerful nation in the planet. President Obama, first African American President of United States, had to overcome early childhood challenges and social and racial prejudices to reach the highest office. He brought stability to the crumbling US economy and there by avoided global recession. He is also working hard to avoid wars and bring peace among nations.

What make all these people tick? What's their life mantra? If we look at their life history, all of them have come up in life through hard times. All are great visionaries and outstanding communicators and devoted their life for a common cause; to serve the humanity. These are universal citizens and their actions transcend geographical boundaries. Let's pick some lessons out of their lives and follow them to make the earth a better place to live.

Digital Twins

Off late, I have been sharing some views on digital technology and how that is disrupting old business models and transforming human lives around the world. The man-machine interactions and near real-time availability of large data sets are opening new vistas in the industrial world. And, artificial intelligence, machine learning, and smart things promise an intelligent future.

The concept of 'digital twins' was introduced by Dr. Michael Grieves of University of Michigan while he was working in collaboration with John Vickers of NASA. Industry giant GE is taking this concept to new heights. Gartner predicts 'digital twin' among top 10 strategic technology trends for 2017. What's Digital Twin? Digital twins refer to computerized companions of physical assets that can be used for various purposes. The concept of the digital twin requires three elements: the physical product in real space, its digital twin in virtual space and the information that links the two. Digital twins use data from Sensors installed on physical objects to represent their near real-time status, working condition or position.

One example of digital twins can be the use of 3D modeling to create a digital companion for the physical object. It can be used to view the status of the actual physical object, which provides a way to project physical objects into the digital world. For example, when sensors collect data from a connected device, the sensor data can be used to update a "digital twin" copy of the device's state in real time. The digital twin is meant to be an up-to-date and accurate copy of the physical object's properties and states, including shape, position, gesture, status and motion.
In another context, Digital twin can be also used for monitoring, diagnostics, and prognostics. In this field, sensory data is sufficient for building digital twins. These models help to improve the outcome of prognostics by using and archiving historical information of physical assets and perform a comparison between fleets of geographically distributed machines.

Therefore, complex prognostics and Intelligent Maintenance System platforms can leverage the use of digital twins in finding the root cause of issues and improve productivity. Digital twins of physical assets combined with digital representations of facilities and environments as well as people, businesses and processes will enable an increasingly detailed digital representation of the real world for simulation, analysis and control.

While the digital twin was initially introduced in manufacturing industries, the applications will quickly grow in all areas of human endeavor; healthcare, retail, banking and finance to name a few. Government and business organizations who adapt non-linear strategies would get benefited immensely with the new approach.

Corporate World - Do You Really Care?

Recent suicide deaths of Anthony Bourdain and Kate Spade, two top celebrities who were adored by millions send shock waves to society at large.

My heart sunk on the sad death of Anthony Bourdain. I really enjoyed watching/listening to this wonderful man. To most of the people that knew him or knew of him, Bourdain was simply strikingly, delightfully good with words. Though his focus was within the world of food, he could speak eloquently and powerfully on nearly any topic, from Armenian genocide to working in restaurants to American politics to omelets. Likewise, fashion designer Kate Spade who created the must-have handbag of the 1990s and turned it into an accessories empire adored by millions also took her life. She was always a very excitable little girl and I felt all the stress/pressure of her brand may have flipped the switch where she eventually became full-on manic depressive.

I shared these two tragic events to highlight even a bigger issue in the corporate world. The stress and pressures of the corporate world are extremely high. While we speak of corporate social responsibility, most organizations, barring few, do not really care about the wellbeing of their employees. I've served in the defense forces as an officer and I can clearly relate this difference. The armed forces around the world pay special attention to both physical and mental health issues and that's why they are able to undertake tasks which are seemingly daunting to normal beings.

The suicide rates are on the rise in the developed countries (The US reported a 30% high in the past two decades) and the modern day pressures adding to this new phenomenon. The mere focus on revenue targets and program delivery and execution would not help in the long run. Clearly, there should be more open communication to understand the overall wellbeing of employees in an organization. Clearly just because someone's life appears good on the outside, doesn't mean all is well in their moments beyond the public eye.

I do have an appeal to all parties- the employees and leaders. Please create more open communication. If someone is not performing at the same level, please try to find out what's going on in his or her life without breaking the privacy protocol. If someone is in trouble, please seek help. Mental illness, depression, or anxiety is no more a taboo.

Let's all start with every conversation (corporate or otherwise) with a genuine inquiry of the personal wellbeing. Despite all the day to day challenges, we all live in a beautiful world. Let's allow everyone enjoy this world to its fullest extent.

If anyone is struggling right now, please contact the Suicide Prevention Lifeline or call 1-800-273-TALK (8255) or the many other professional mental health care agencies.

Breaking the Glass Ceiling

The effect of culture on leadership strategies, goals, and behavior of business organizations have been a major focus of leadership researchers. The current study is a significant addition to the broader field of leadership studies involving ethnic and socio-cultural aspects of a prominent but understudied population in leadership literature.

Asian Indian immigrants play a vital role in the US Information Technology Industry. However, no extensive research has been published on Asian Indian techno-immigrants. Study of the available literature indicated a general problem of under-representation of Asian Indian immigrants in IT organizations at high-level leadership positions in the United States, though there is a significant presence at junior levels within these establishments.

Despite the perceived glass ceiling, several Asian Indian immigrants have achieved notable success and attained high-level leadership positions in the U.S. IT industry. The current hermeneutic phenomenological study focuses on understudied areas within scholarly literature. The study explored the lived experience of Asian Indian immigrants in high-level leadership positions in the U.S. Information Technology industry and the impact of their racial and sociocultural identity on being high-level leaders in the U.S. IT sector.

The current phenomenological inquiry uncovered six essential themes from the data analysis that includes: (1) socio-cultural experience, (2) advanced technology skills, (3) leadership competency, (4) ethnic identity and assimilation, (5) personal and family sacrifices and (6) sustainment of motivation. And, the study provides an in-depth insight of the lived experiences, perspectives, and thoughts of IT leaders of Asian Indian origin about winning themes and address "glass ceiling" issues that limit the growth of aspiring leaders.

How the "Big History" Shaping my Thinking and Writing.

I took a forced sabbatical from my writing activities while focusing on my Doctoral dissertation. The focus paid off and I have successfully defended my dissertation in February 2018. I'm back into my writing gig.

I do have several areas of interest including, technology, leadership, spirituality, running to name a few. Recently I got an additional area of interest, the Big History influenced by the writings and teachings of Professor David Christian from San Diego State University in California and Macquarie University, Australia. In my opinion, learning the "Big History" (which starts with the Big Bang that happened 13.8 Billion years) and in particular human history is an essential requirement on our transformational journey which will help to shape the future in a positive way.

Maybe it's a coincidence that I wrote about this topic on the day of passing (March 13, 2018) of Stephen Hawking, the author of 'A Brief History of Time'. Hawking was considered one of the leading voices in science because of his extensive research and work related to understanding the universe. A tribute to the legend! Here is the last inspiring message from Stephen Hawing to mankind. https://www.youtube.com/watch?v=VYxjumUhji0 Watch for this column for future readings on technology, leadership, and exciting articles on the topic.

Ingredients of High Performance

What are the key ingredients of high performance? Essentially, just two:

1. Structure
2. Habits

This is equally applicable in personal life as well as corporate settings.

In personal settings, structure put you in the correct framework and habits take you to the end game successfully.

In corporate settings, effective leaders clearly articulate the structure; a strategic framework of mission, vision and values, strategic goals, and the "critical few" measurable priorities. These leaders also master three personal habits of high performance; direction, evidence, and execution and make it a point to execute them repeatedly.

Finally, 'what you are, what you repeatedly do'. Create a structure that helps high performance and makes it a habit to perform repeatedly at the highest level.

Coaching for Leaders

I'm a practicing leader and a leadership researcher. My previous article on leadership drew a lot of attention with several thousand views, shares, and likes. That has motivated me to write a re-jointer to the previous article. Some of the thoughts here are based on my field experience and also based on academic research on the topic.

Leader's job is never easy, however, they make or break organizations. My first advice to any leader is that 'be a leader and not a boss'. Be empathetic, use softer words, but be hard to the task. Please do not use big management jargons, explain the requirements in simple terms and validate to make sure that your team understands them well. Set high goals and higher standards and also live by those standards. Admit faults, be human, accept team's mistakes and show them the way they can improve. Address the issues and not challenge the people bringing them to your attention.

Personal integrity and value system must be on top of the agenda of the leader. Walk the talk, people watch your actions, not your words. Be responsive to your team, they are reaching out to you because they are seeking your advice. If you act busy, you will lose a loyal team member or colleague.

Men and women have different demands and are wired differently. Women can handle multi-tasking more efficiently. They are like radar, can scan a wide range of issues at a given time. They can handle stress better than men. You may argue on this topic, but multiple research shows this aspect. So, engage more women in your leadership roles. Men are better at handling one task at a time. They can be laser-focused on a particular task. Employ them wisely in roles where they can bring better results.

Finally, learn to accept feedback and criticisms with a positive mindset. The criticism would outweigh compliment for most of the time. If you are aligned with these thoughts, you are into a successful leadership track. Good luck!

A Constant Leadership Reminder

Leadership can be defined as the process of influencing people, as leader confirms that objectives get achieved by efforts and coordination of all employees and for which he motivate people and also ensures the culture which is apt to perform. Leadership is a group event. Leaders use different styles with subordinates to influence the situation and make an impact on employees. Therefore they impact the performance.

Best fitted behavior to people and organization will result in increasing the performance. Leadership paradigms are being changed and the organization does not have the leaders matching this new thought of subordinates they face problems to reach objectives. Such leaders are productive but only for short span. Therefore the requirement of leadership with changed pattern and values of employees and fitness to the organization should also change to ensure desired performance. Continuously organization requirements replicate the fact that leadership is very crucial in any kind of organization. Imperfect leadership may encounter various problems whereas perfect leadership may lead to smooth functioning, motivated employees and overall effectiveness in the performance of the organization, without changing other factors in the organization.

Leadership is always being vital and vivid from time to time and organization to organization.

One leader may produce better results in a specific organization but may not be so efficient for other organization. Reasons could be many for instance his working style, his people interaction pattern, the fitness of leader with the organization structure; culture; and other related factors or may be alone his personality. But for sure it does make an influence on the overall effectiveness and performance of the organization. Finally, leadership is a journey. Keep an open mind to learn at every stage. Please continue to disseminate the leadership message to your leaders, peers, and followers. Let's all collectively work for a better tomorrow!

Live the "Future" Today

One day my loved one had a medical emergency. I was hard hit by the new development. While it was painful, it also opened up new possibilities, a new realization and a future of blissful moments in my life. All these years, I never fully acknowledged the real value of what I had.

If we don't enjoy what we have today, we'll never get to enjoy what's in future. So, give the future to the present and enjoy the moment.

Skeptical Cat

The other day I was listening to a keynote on YouTube by Dr. Julian Sanchez from John Deere Technology Innovation Center. He interestingly brought up the story of the skeptical cats. He joked that you should not have the compliance team as your skeptical cats. Jokes aside, this has an important message.

It is always good to have skeptical cats on your team, except that they should not derail your project. While skeptical, they should lean towards successful execution of the program. The idea behind skeptical cats is to collect opposing viewpoints that open the door for more discussions. The emphasis should be on mutual, evidence-based discourse while exploring issues and challenging misinformation. A continuing discussion of evidence-based strategies gives us new tools as we seek open dialogue that produces meaningful output.

I had personally come across similar experiences and always encouraged opposing views and skeptical cats in the room. So, next time when you come across such people in your program use it as an opportunity to validate your assumptions and strategy. Also, please make sure that they don't derail your plans.

Leadership and Self-Management

The first person you must lead is YOU. Effective leadership starts from within – with self-management. On the foundation, then it provides connection and facilitates learning. Constant learning through iterative experimentation and transparent communication transforms the organization to produce industry game-changing innovation.

Dr. Sunnie Giles, based on her extensive research in neuroscience and social science, summarized the following leadership traits that bring in dramatic and permanent results:

1. Masters self-management
2. Provides safety for others
3. Facilitates differentiation
4. Creates connection and belonging in the organization
5. Facilitates effective learning
6. Promotes growth at the edge of chaos

Integrity, ethics and high moral standards are something we look at the leaders. To get there one must master self-management and lead by example.

Business Optimization Approaches in a Global Context

The multinational corporation (MNC), often seen as a primary agent of globalization, is taking on a new form, one that is promising for both business and society. From a business perspective, this new kind of enterprise is best understood as "global" rather than "multinational". The shift from Multinational Corporation to globally integrated enterprise has assumed two distinct forms. The first has involved changes in where companies produce things; the second, changes in who produces them. Until recently, companies generally chose to produce goods close to where they sold them. As a consequence, most foreign investments targeted specific foreign markets. Today, overseas investments continue to be made with a view to gaining access to important sources of foreign demand, but companies are investing more to change the way they supply the entire global market. The global integration of production cuts costs and taps new sources of skills and knowledge.

Heretofore, the corporation was seen as a collection of country-based subsidiaries, business units, or product lines. Now the spread of outsourcing is encouraging companies to view themselves as an array of specialized components: procurement, manufacturing, research, sales, distribution, and so on. For each of these components, the global integration of operations is forcing companies to choose where they want the work to be performed and whether they want it performed in-house or by an outside partner. The corporation, then, is emerging as a combination of various functions and skills -- some tightly bound and some loosely coupled -- and it integrates these components of business activity and production on a global basis to produce goods and services for its customers. This simple change in the corporation's purpose and mission has many ramifications.

Systemic changes

The globally integrated enterprise will require fundamentally different approaches to production, distribution, and work-force deployment. This is already happening with leading companies like IBM. Because new technology and business models are allowing companies to treat their different functions and operations as component pieces, firms can pull those pieces apart and put them back together again in new combinations, based on strategic judgments about which operations the company wants to excel at and which it thinks are best suited to its partners.

These decisions are not simply a matter of offloading noncore activities, nor are they mere labor arbitrage. They are about actively managing different operations, expertise, and capabilities so as to open the enterprise up in multiple ways, allowing it to connect more intimately with partners, suppliers, and customers. The extraordinary growth of service firms like IBM Global Services provide specialized expertise makes this possible. New forms of collaboration are everywhere: from increasingly complex intercompany production networks to the open-source software movement, which has helped transform the traditional model of innovation. Today, innovation is not led by lone inventors in their garrets but is the product of a collaborative process that also combines technological and marketing expertise. And such open approaches affect far more than software and IT: they also apply to education, governance, and many industries.

Opportunities and challenges
The globally integrated enterprise can deliver enormous economic benefits to both developed and developing nations. The integration of the work force in developing countries into

global systems of production is already raising living standards, improving working conditions, and creating more jobs in those countries. Small and medium-sized businesses everywhere, particularly, are benefiting: as new services -- from back-office administration to sales support -- create infrastructures once only affordable to large organizations, these businesses can now participate in the global economy. The opportunities for more such stories are enormous. But shifting to the model of globally integrated enterprises also presents big challenges for leaders in every sector of society. The very fact that so many more people all over the world are gaining equal access to the production process and the marketplace means much more trade and competition. Although this will create wealth and opportunity, it will also bring disruption and fear, both of which could threaten global integration. Legitimate concerns about job loss and skill shortages must be addressed in realistic and constructive ways.

Global collaboration

Government leaders will find in business willing partners to reform health care and education, secure the world's trade lanes and electronic commerce, train and enable the displaced and dispossessed, grapple with environmental problems and infectious diseases, and tackle the myriad other challenges that globalization raises. The globally integrated enterprise is a promising new actor on the world stage. Now leaders in business, government, education, and all of civil society must learn about its emerging dynamics and help it mature in ways that will contribute to social, economic, and human progress around the planet.

Marketing Optimization

In today's very competitive marketplace, a strategy that insures a consistent approach to offering product or service in a way that will outsell the competition is critical, Center for Business Planning (2006). However, in concert with defining the marketing strategy one must also have a well-defined methodology for the day to day process of implementing it. It is of little value to have a strategy if the organization lacks either the resources or the expertise to implement it.

There are two major components to marketing strategy:
1. How your enterprise will address the competitive marketplace
2. How you will implement and support your day to day operations.

It is now a well-accepted paradigm that measurement is essential to marketing. Marketing professionals at all levels and in all industries want to know the impact of their efforts. Whenever possible, the key measurement should be return on investment (ROI). While the balanced scorecard approach legitimately emphasizes the need to look at a wide variety of metrics to understand what is driving marketing performance, ultimately what is important is the bottom line. Measurement, of course, is not an end in itself. The purpose of measurement is to drive marketing decisions that will increase ROI. Thus, there is now a widely seen emphasis on marketing or ROI "optimization.". This article attempts to sort out these many options into a few understandable categories and explain why each is relevant and important.

Types of Marketing Optimization

Marketers have a very wide choice of tools and methods available to help in decision making. These range from proprietary commercial tools to widely used standard methodologies. While any grouping will certainly ignore some important distinctions, the four categories are identified as:

- Program Metrics
- Mix Models Optimization
- Targeting Optimization
- Marketing Simulation

This section defines the tools and methodologies of each category. Each of these types of optimization technique is potentially valuable.

Program Metrics

Program metrics simply refers to the practice of measuring the performance of individual marketing programs or activities and using these measurements to drive decisions about whether to expand or curtail the programs. Many metrics can be relevant, depending on the type of program under consideration.

Mix Models/Optimization

The past decade has seen the emergence of a sizable industry devoted to estimating marketing mix models and providing marketing optimization tools based upon the mix model results. This is especially prevalent in the consumer packaged goods (CPG) industry.

Briefly, a marketing mix model is a statistical regression analysis that quantifies the relationship between sales and the key factors that drive sales such as advertisement media weight and mix, consumer promotions, trade support, pricing, competitive activity and seasonality.

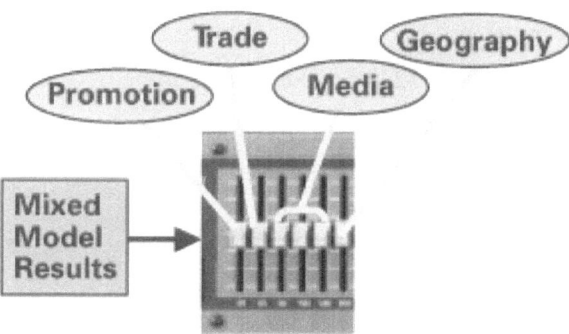

Figure 2: Mix Model Optimization

Targeting Optimization

One of the current major thrusts of marketing is customer relationship management (CRM) and one-to- one marketing. In a modern marketing organization, implementation of these programs requires a customer-centric data mart and sophisticated software and statistical analysis techniques. A third type of marketing optimization tool supports these systems by providing optimal individual-level targeting of marketing communications and offers.

Marketing Simulation

The final type of optimization technique provides guidance by building simulation models of the marketing process. An effective simulation tool must capture both the qualitative elements of the marketing process (what channels, products, offers, etc. are in use or under consideration and what structures are available for integrating these elements into a cohesive marketing process) and the quantitative measures of how customers and prospects respond to marketing activities at each stage of the marketing process

Characterizing Optimization Techniques

The categories described suggest a characterization of marketing optimization techniques along two dimensions: strategic versus tactical and flexible versus specialized. There is no suggestion, of course, that strategic is always better than tactical or that flexible is always better than specialized. Each technique is valuable for specific purposes. These characteristics are summarized in Figure 3.

Charteristic	Description	Advantages
Strategic	• Addresses high-level issues across marketing categories • Addresses marketing program structure and integration • Looks at major changes, not incremental shifts	• Major impact on marketing success possible
Tactical	• Concerns implementation of existing or identified programs	• Easy to implement • Quick payoff
Flexible	• Can address a wide variety of issues and marketing elements • Can be customized for each implementation	• No limit on what issues can be addressed
Specialized	• Designed for specific issues or marketing elements	• Easy to implement • Track record of success in similar situations • Takes advantage of special circumstances

Figure 3: Marketing Optimization Characteristics

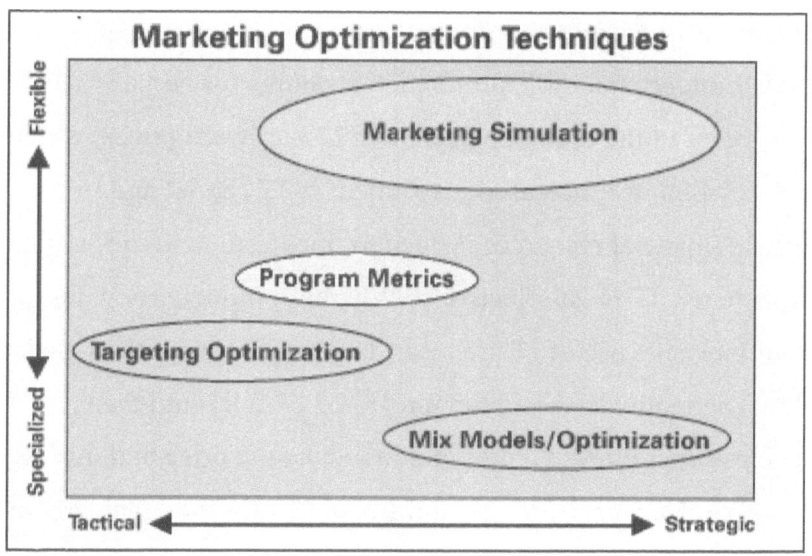

Figure 4: Types and Uses of Marketing Optimization Techniques

Strategic techniques should be of particular interest to higher level marketing executives who must make budget allocation decisions across categories of marketing activities. Tactical tools benefit managers who are in the trenches executing marketing programs. Specialized tools are very good for the specific tasks for which they were designed but flexibility is required to capture the unique and changing aspects of some markets. Each marketing manager should understand the techniques most helpful for their specific objectives.

Role of IT in business optimization

Global integration of IT production accounts for perhaps 10 to 30 percent of the dramatic decline in IT hardware prices, which was key both for increased investment in IT capital and to release financial resources needed to transform activities within firms to use IT most effectively. Whereas productivity gains from intensive use of IT are clear, large segments of the US and global economy have not yet integrated IT fully into their business operations. Continuing to reduce the price and making the IT package easier to use and a better fit for the organization that buys it are necessary to deepen and spread more widely the use of IT and the associated transformation of activities.

Nascent globalization of software and services, if it takes the pattern of price declines that enable development of higher valued-added and sector-specific applications (as has been the case with globalization of IT hardware), could help vault these hurdles. The result would be IT diffusion to and more extensive transformation of sectors and firm sizes that have lagged in terms of productivity growth, as well as deeper integration of IT software and services into the sectors that have already enjoyed significant productivity gains based on hardware. The resulting second wave of productivity growth could be even greater than the one experienced in the in the early 2000s.

Going forward, the globalization of software and IT services and the movement of some jobs abroad reduce the price of "components." (Software and services have components just as hardware does.) In the United States, the jobs will be to design, tailor, and implement IT packages for a broader range of industries and size of firms as well as to deepen the integration of IT into firms that already have it. Suppose that global integration of software and services yielded price declines of 20 percent (using the average of the results from the IT hardware research). Since the demand for software and IT services is more price elastic than for IT hardware, the potential increase in investment, productivity growth, and job creation from the globalization of IT services and software is even greater than that experienced in the 1990s from the globalization of IT hardware. Indeed, this second wave of productivity growth and the associated economy wide gains *depend* on deeper integration of IT and transformation of more sectors of the US economy and the workers who can engender and partake of these changes.

Conclusion

In this strategic marketing and financial leadership plan, this learner has attempted to discuss various optimization strategies from organizational standpoint; both financial optimization and marketing optimization. What has become evident is the importance of these two critical entities within a business organization. The study also brought out the changes in paradigm in the new world order, the impact of globalization and ever increasing role of IT as an enabler in this context. Several qualitative and quantitative approaches were also discussed with detailed focus on marketing optimization strategies.

Globally integrated organizations are seen as the next generation which optimizes operations and reduce cost by cutting down non-revenue generating expenses. Globalization of IT hardware played an important role in business expansion. In order to return to the economic performance of the 1990s, the early IT adopters will have to deepen IT investment and transformation, and the process of IT investment and transformation will have to be extended to the sectors of the global economy that did not participate in the productivity growth of the early 2000s—among them, health services, construction, and small and medium businesses. Globalization of software and services will entail some jobs being done abroad but will result in lower prices for the overall IT package. The resulting greater use of IT and transformation of activities throughout the economy will propel the United States toward a second wave of faster productivity growth that at the same time yields a greater demand for IT-related jobs spread throughout the economy.

The article discussed at length on the integration of global economy and business operations in a global context by sharing Globally Integrated Enterprise model. The article brings in challenging questions to senior leadership. Are they looking for only financial imperative? What does this ask about leadership role of executive? In a fast changing world, organizations are looking for transformational leaders who have the vision to translate the organizations into high performing cultures in a globally integrated enterprise. This is a challenging task worth emulating.

Author Biography

Dr. Saju Skaria is a senior business executive with extensive Information Technology background with a career spanning over 30 years. Currently, he is a Senior Director at Tata Consultancy Services (TCS), a Global Leader in IT Services, Consulting, Technology and Digital Solutions. In his role, Dr. Skaria is responsible for IT business with US Manufacturing Companies in Aerospace, Automotive, Process, and Industrial segments.

Before joining TCS, Dr. Skaria has served at Xerox Corporation as Vice President and Client Managing Director. Dr. Skaria started his career with the Indian Air Force in the Engineering branch as a commissioned officer and worked closely with various defense, civil, and R&D establishments while in India. Dr. Skaria moved to the US in 2001 and held leadership business roles progressively at IBM, Infosys, and Xerox while serving various fortune hundred clients before his current position with TCS.

Dr. Saju Skaria holds Doctorate in Business Administration with focus on Leadership and Information Technology. He has an Undergraduate Degree in Mechanical Engineering, Master's Degree in Aerospace Engineering, and an MBA in Marketing.

Dr. Skaria is a Marathon runner, avid reader, technology and leadership researcher, speaker, and blogger. He is a US citizen with extensive international travel and business experience and consults with multiple fortune one hundred clients.

Dr. Saju Skaria lives in Phoenix, Arizona, USA along with his beautiful wife, Shiny. They have two adult children Rinku and Robin, both university students. He can be contacted through email: SajuSkaria@gmail.com or through his US mobile number: (602) 758 9982

www.ingramcontent.com/pod-product-compliance
Lightning Source LLC
Chambersburg PA
CBHW031414210526
45464CB00005B/1873